Self-Management - Understanding Behavioral Competency

Copyright © 2014 Gian Paolo Roma
All rights reserved.

For permission requests contact the author:
Gian Paolo Roma
RomaGianPaolo@gmail.com
romag@sunybroome.edu

Gian Paolo Roma
SUNY Broome Community College
PO Box 1017
Binghamton, NY 13902

Friendsville Publishing Group
Self-Management - Understanding Behavioral Competency
Gian Paolo Roma

ISBN-13: 978-1494474256
ISBN-10: 1494474255

Printed in the United States of America.

Cover Design by Ursula Roma
Cover Fonts: Futura & Helvetica
Interior Design by Gian Paolo Roma
Interior Font: Times Roman

A College Success Course

Self-Management
Understanding Behavioral Competency

First Edition

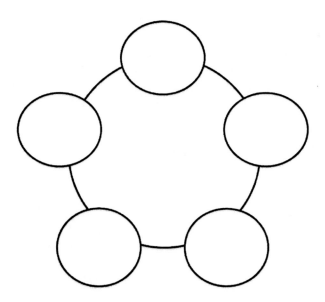

Gian Paolo Roma

Self-Management - Understanding Behavioral Competency
Friendsville Publishing Group
Gian Paolo Roma - © 2014 - All Rights Reserved

Dedications

For my wife, Arlene, and our daughters; Alli and Cori.

For my parents; Kari and Emilio - my siblings; Chip, Ursi, Axie, Nick - my aunts; Pat, Cathy, Dorothy - my nephews; Paolo, Sam, and Max – my nieces Shari, Dayna, and Melissa - my in-laws Helen, Murray, Doreen, and Steven.

For my friends, colleagues, and associates; Chris Adams, Dan Avery, Francis Battisti, Rick Behr, Dean Bender, Dave Benninger, Stew Brouse, Katie Bucci, John Bunnell, Irene Byrnes, Scott Calloway, Mark Caron, Tony Cherone, Gary Cuccio, Tom DeCelle, Dominic DePersis, Bob Dewing, Tera Doty-Blance, Matt Dowd, Scott Corley, Kevin Drumm, Doug Garner, Judy Giblin, Marty Guzzi, Rachael Hagerman, Jeff Hatala, Tony Heyman, Deb Hibbard, Robert Hurley, Jeff Jurik, Tom Kanick, Mike Keenan, Michael Kinney, Julie Klepfer, Hal Koster, Mike Kuryla, John Kuzma, Debbie Lake, Jon Layish, Victor Lamoureux, Annette LeRoy, Kelly Ligikis, Julie Lin, Regina Losinger, Brian Loy, Jerry Loy, Joan Lubar, Mary McCarthy, Dan McGurgan, Meghan McGuiness, Kathleen McKenna, Fred Mellert, Carla and Dave Michalak, Michael McKimmy, Beth Mollen, Loreta Paniccia, Charles Petrolawicz, Joyce Prindle, Chris Rollo, Pat O'Bryan, Joe O'Conner, Diane O'Heron, Louis Osman, Maryanne Parvel, Michelle Perricone, Jan Pitera, Robert Reh, Margherita Rossi, Tom Rossi, Mark Ryan, Darin Schmidt, Bob Schulteiz, Mid Semple, Celia Slom, Joe Spence, Sheila Steinbach, Sharon Steinberg, Anita Stewart, Lisa Strahley, Cheryl Sullivan, Corinne Surdey, Greg Talley, George and Mary Terela, Phil Testa, Jan Toraason, Joo Phaik Tschang, Greg Vimont, William Vinck, Andrea Wade, Wes Warren, Nate Walz, Kerry Weber, Denise Wells, Mary Whittaker, Diane Whitehead, Rey Wojdat, Glen Wood, Jennifer Woltjen, Sandra Wright, and Jason Zbock.

<u>Thanks to Reviewers:</u>

Jack Duffy, PhD
Dalhousie University
Professor Emeritus
Rowe School of Business

Dina Naples-Layish, PhD
Binghamton University
School of Management

Brenda Gainer, PhD
York University
Schulich School of Business

Margaret Reed, PhD
University of Cincinnati
Lindner College of Business

William R. Hollister, PhD
SUNY Broome Community College
Department of Biology

Table of Contents

Introduction

*"If you are to be, you must begin by assuming responsibility.
You alone are responsible for every moment of your life, for every one of your acts."*

~ Antoine de Saint-Exupery

The non-graduation rate of college students in the United States is estimated to be somewhere between 30% and 50% depending on who is doing the counting. Whatever the real number actually is, it is a troubling number that highlights the need for students to be more resilient, prepared, and effective at reaching their goals.

How can you better prepare yourself to succeed in this increasingly demanding, changing, and competitive world? One way is to learn and practice the basic behaviors and traits necessary to achieve your goals. For most people, *genuine* success and achievement, academic, social, career, financial, or otherwise, is earned and is a function of their own behavioral conduct, rather than a result of the circumstances into which they were born. *True* self-confidence is an *outcome or result* of sustained effort made over time to achieve a goal and cannot be inherited or acquired by those unwilling or unable to endure the rigors required for *genuine* success. Although family members, teachers, advisors, and friends can help you formulate plans on how best to achieve your goals, ultimately *you* are the only person that can turn your plans into reality.

Behavioral competency can be characterized as a basic understanding and consistent practice of a set of skills that nurtures trust. Trust is having "confident reliance" on another party in situations involving vulnerability or risk[1].

> *Behaviorally competent people
> comprehend how their own behavior affects trust.*

They have an emotional and intellectual appreciation of the value of trust in goal achievement, and an understanding that their own actions, deeds, and words can affect trust. Trust is the outcome of competent behavior.

A simple definition of Self-Management (SM) is …

> *the ability to achieve one's own goals in a trustworthy manner.*

We can think in the abstract of individual behavior as either *strengthening* or *weakening* trust - or *"healthy"* or *"unhealthy"* respectively. *Healthy behaviors* are defined as those that strengthen trust connections and create goodwill between people. Examples of healthy behaviors are showing up on time, working hard, appreciating others, and adapting to difficult or changing

---

[1] Hurley, Robert. "The Decision to Trust: How Leaders Create High Trust Organization", *Jossey-Bass*, 2011, p.25

situations. *Unhealthy behaviors* such as lack of effort and accountability, being unreliable, disrespecting others, using poor judgment, and making reckless decisions, can cause others to feel upset, frustrated, scared, and angry, which can destroy goodwill and cooperation. *Unhealthy behaviors* usually require other people [e.g. supervisors, professors, parents, advisors, family-members, police, etc.] to intervene to prevent negative outcomes from occurring. Society's most extreme examples of behavioral intervention are jail and the death penalty. Lesser degrees of unhealthy behavior also erode trust between people.

The main purpose of this book is to help you achieve your goals by clarifying the SM behaviors and traits that foster trust and success, and to provide "how to" help in applying them to your own life. This book is organized into five SM Units, [communication, choice, commitment, coping, and consideration], which are called the 5Cs of Self-Management.

5Cs of Self-Management Model

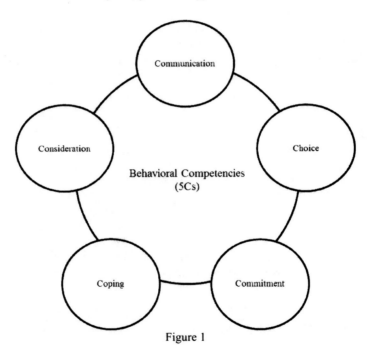

Figure 1

Certain behaviors communicate certain character traits that are linked to specific types of trust. For instance, patterns of behavior that are rude and uncaring towards others expose an individual's inconsiderate nature. The outcome of inconsiderate behavior toward others is relationship mistrust. Whereas behaviors like procrastination or laziness reveals commitment-related issues which would translate into activity mistrust.

Behaviors make visible what is trustworthy and untrustworthy about people's character. SM requires that people organize and control their own behavioral reactions through self-imposed, trustworthy rules of conduct. SM focuses on learning to control one's own emotional, intellectual, and physical reactions to life's events.

The idea that certain behaviors communicate certain types of trust works well in assessing or diagnosing behavioral performance. Behavior and trust are both multi-dimensional. Each of the 5Cs correlates directly to a specific type of trust or trust category [see Table 1.1]. Looking at trust through the 5C framework provides trust definitions for each trust category and links trust to specific behaviors.

5Cs of SM	*Trust Category*	*Trust Definition*
Communication	Communication-Based	Trust a person to convey messages that are appropriate.
Choices	Judgment-Based	Trust a person to prioritize important matters ahead of unimportant matters.
Consideration	Relationship-Based	Trust a person to show thoughtful concern for others.
Commitment	Activity-Based	Trust a person to meet obligations to others.
Coping	Situation-Based	Trust a person to handle and adapt to difficult, changing, and complex circumstances.

Table 1.1

It is also possible to be trustworthy in one *trust category* but not another, such as demonstrating commitment to work, while at the same time, being very inconsiderate toward coworkers. Keep in mind that an individual can be trustworthy to one activity but not another, such as showing commitment to partying with friends or playing sports, but not to academics. The behaviorally competent individual can be trusted in all five trust categories simultaneously, not just one or two. He or she communicates appropriately, makes good choices, shows thoughtful concern for others, meets his or her obligations to others, and handles difficult, changing, and complex situations effectively.

Why are behavioral understanding and trust so important? There is a growing body of evidence that suggests that many people [young and old] go through life without giving any serious thought or having a depth of understanding about their own behavior and how it can affect their lives. For instance, a recent study published in the Harvard Business Review found that "98% of workers polled reported experiencing uncivil behavior" in the workplace[2]. This is significant because behaviors like incivility that undermine the dignity, confidence, and self-worth of other people can weaken or possibly even sever the trust connections that bind people together. Once trust is broken, unhappiness, conflict, and polarization often are the result, any of which can compromise or destroy goodwill between people.

Many of the biggest problems we face can be traced back to untrustworthy behavior that has destroyed people's willingness to cooperate with one another.

What do you think?

How do you treat people that you don't trust? Do you treat them differently than people you do trust? Would you hire someone you didn't trust? Why or why not?

_____

_____

_____

_____

_____

_____

_____

Although academic ability is important, it does not guarantee academic success. Academic ability is a function of behavioral skills. Students who attend class, do their homework and study tend to do much better than those that do not. Each year, many smart students drop out of college because they are unable to manage their own behavior. Think about your own behavior and how it relates to your own success and complete as honestly as you can the following self-assessment.

---

[2] Porath, Christine, and Pearson, Christine, "The Price of Incivility", *Harvard Business Review* Jan-Feb 2013, p.114

Self-Management (SM)
A Self-Assessment

Do you "agree or disagree" with the following statements? For every statement that you disagree with, please briefly explain why you disagree.

	Action Statement	Agree/Disagree
1	I spend between 10 and 20 hours, outside of class, on my schoolwork [e.g. doing homework, studying, or preparing for tests].	
2	I challenge myself to practice and understand subjects that I find difficult or I do not understand well.	
3	I always get all of my work done, no matter how long it takes.	
4	I go out with friends only after my academic work is completed.	
5	I don't miss class and am always on time.	
6	I am ready to work and prepared for every class.	
7	I almost always earn high grades [A's or B's] or marks in my classes.	
8	I am comfortable in college and like communicating and meeting new people	
9	When I do poorly or when I don't understand something, I try harder by putting in more time on that subject.	
10	I can juggle large amounts of responsibility at school, work, and home and still produce high quality work.	

11	I can figure out how to do almost any subject, if I put my mind and effort into it.	
12	I always try to be courteous, even when I don't need to be.	
13	I consider the other person and can find common ground when I am in a dispute.	
14	I am careful not to harm people with my words, even when I get frustrated.	
15	I challenge myself to help bring order to different situations, even when things do not go my way.	
16	I always try to make ethically sound decisions.	
17	I prioritize important matters in front of less important matters when I make decisions.	
18	I adjust my behavior depending on who I am interacting with.	
19	I always think about what I am saying or doing before I talk or act.	
20	I am interested in what others have to say, even when I disagree with their points of view.	

Now transfer your answers [agree or disagree] for each statement into the corresponding space in the Self-Management Mapping Table shown on the next page.

Self-Management
Behavior Mapping Table

Item	Agree/ Disagree	Behavior	5Cs
1		Time	Commitment
2		Deliberate Practice	Commitment
3		Effort	Commitment
4		Delayed Gratification	Commitment
5		Reliability	Commitment
6		Preparedness	Commitment
7		Quality	Commitment
8		Change	Coping
9		Adversity	Coping
10		Capacity	Coping
11		Capability	Coping
12		Courteousness	Consideration
13		Negotiating	Consideration
14		Courteous	Consideration
15		Helpfulness	Consideration
16		Ethical	Choice
17		Judgment	Choice
18		Audience	Communication
19		Message	Communication
20		Listening	Communication

Table 1.3

Johann Wolfgang Von Goethe wrote more than 200 years ago, "Behavior is the mirror in which everyone shows their image." Your behavior communicates a great deal about you. The SM Behavior Mapping Table shows you how the 5Cs relate to your behavior. Your academic performance [good or bad] will be largely the result of your behavior. Because certain behaviors lead to better academic performance than others, it is appropriate and necessary for you to study and understand the relationship between your behavior and your performance. Use this book to help you develop your own strategies for improving your academic performance by turning your "disagrees" into "agrees." Understanding and controlling your own behavior will affect not only your academic future, but also your life after graduation.

Self-Management - Understanding Behavioral Competency
Friendsville Publishing Group
Gian Paolo Roma - © 2014 - All Rights Reserved

Unit 1
Communications

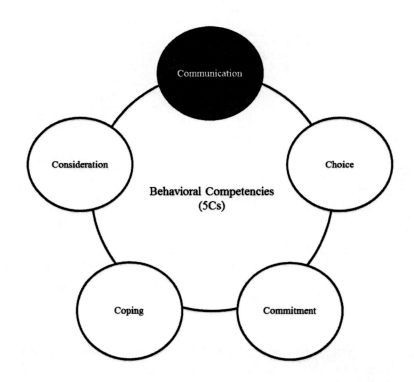

Self-Management - Understanding Behavioral Competency
Friendsville Publishing Group
Gian Paolo Roma - © 2014 - All Rights Reserved

Understanding Communications

"The most important thing in communication is hearing what isn't said."

~ Peter F. Drucker

Everything we say and do communicates facts and information about ourselves that influences how others see us. Our actions and words profoundly affect others' beliefs about and actions towards us. What and how we communicate helps others determine our underlying nature, and whether or not they want to associate with us. It is through our own communications that people "figure us out." People decide to like us, trust us, hire us, or even marry us based on what and how we communicate.

Most of what individuals communicate every moment of every day has very little to do with words. Research shows that only about 10 percent of communication involves words, written and verbal[3]. When you think about it, it's astounding that humans are the only life form on the planet that use words to communicate. Words help humans explain and understand the context and meaning of the world, but they are only a small part of how people communicate.

A simple thought experiment can illustrate how this works. The feelings and emotions associated with love are the same around the world; only the words used to name love are completely different. In Czech, its láska; in Russian, любовь, and in Turkish: aşk. The word for love is not the feeling or emotion of being in love. If two people did not speak the same language, would they still be able to communicate a deep affection for one another? Feelings, moods, emotions, and actions all "speak" for themselves. They communicate a great deal without a word.

In fact, more than 90 percent of communication does not involve words[4]. We communicate with our voice inflection and our nonverbal communications, such as our actions and deeds.

What we do and how we do it convey to others our feelings and the kind of person we are. Most importantly, we are not credible when our words are not backed up by our actions. To that extent, our actions and deeds are what is real about us and therefore define who we are to others. They convey information about our true nature, as opposed to our words, which explain only how we might like to be seen. We continually send information nonverbally about our values, ethics, judgment, manner, emotions, friendliness, interest, desire, motivation, attitude, aptitude, dependability, and work ethic. Although our writing and speaking skills are important, nonverbal communication reveals a great deal more about us.

---

[3] Mehrabian, A. and Wiener, M. (1967). Decoding of Inconsistent Communications, *Journal of Personality and Social Psychology*, 6, 109-114

[4] ibid

Since the messages we communicate influence other people's attitudes and behavior towards us, it is important that we proactively assess the appropriateness of our communications and the affect they have on the people we meet.

The focus of this unit is to improve the effectiveness of *your* communications. Its purpose is to aid you in communicating in a way that supports you in achieving your goals. Specifically, we want to try to determine what messages are important to people and ensure that your communications satisfy those requirements. To communicate more effectively you will learn how to A.I.M.E. when you communicate.

Audience:	Identify all audience types with whom you communicate.
Involvement:	Identify how you are involved with each audience type.
Message:	Determine the single most important message that each audience must receive.
Evidence:	Provide behavioral evidence to audience members that your actions and words are aligned with their expectations.

Let us look at each of the four A.I.M.E. elements of effective communication.

Audience

The first step in communicating effectively is to identify the different people with whom you interact and define the characteristics that are unique to each type. We will call the different classes of people "audience types." Gathering detailed information on the characteristics of audience types will put you in a better position to gauge the appropriateness of your communication messages during your interactions. Before we go any further, take a few minutes to jot down some of the difference audience types with whom you interact regularly. Try to make the list as comprehensive as possible.

Audience Types:

1. _____   4. _____

2. _____   5. _____

3. _____   6. _____

Involvement

Now that you have identified the different audience types, let's define how you are involved with each type. For example, it is not enough to say, "I am my parent's child." What does it feel like to be involved with you as a parent, or professor, or employer? What are the drives, goals, and opinions of the different audience types regarding their involvement with you? Involvement looks at whether or not an audience type cares much about the outcomes of your behavioral choices. Some audience types will care a great deal about you and your behavior, and some will not. In general, audience types with a *big stake* in your behavior [i.e., those whose success and or reason for being relies on your behavior] will have high degrees of concern about your behavior. The opposite is also true. Audience types that are not impacted much by your behavior would have lower degrees of concern about your behavior.

What follows is a list of audience types with varying levels of involvement with your behavior.

Parents	The role of the typical parent is to care for and protect offspring while they grow and develop [physically, emotionally, intellectually, and behaviorally]. Most parents show high levels of concern about their children's prospects for health, happiness, fortune, and well-being. Strong feelings of affection [love], support, and loyalty create high levels of concern about behavioral outcomes.
Professors	College and university professors are teachers who educate students at the postsecondary level. One of the primary duties of professors is to assess student subject-matter understanding. Professors use tests, quizzes, oral and written reports, and class participation to gauge the degree of that understanding. Most professors devote a lot of effort to insure that grading outcomes accurately reflect their students' level of understanding.
	Student behaviors [e.g. time spent studying, attending class, doing homework] all influence academic performance. To put it another way, students who study and go to class generally do better than students who do not. Because academic performance relies on behavioral performance, the grade really reflects student proficiency in both areas: academic and behavioral.
Colleges and Universities	Colleges and universities use factors such as grades, academic rigor, and SAT/ACT to measure and compare students in the admissions process. They choose students carefully because student selectivity is one of the main factors used to rate academic institutions. Highly rated schools attract many more students than those that are not, which contributes to

Colleges and Universities [cont.] more stable tuition revenue streams at those institutions. For example, each semester, highly selective schools such as Harvard, Stanford, and MIT are flooded with applications from the highest quality students from around the world. Their tuition revenue streams are much more predictable and steady than colleges that receive fewer applications.

Another factor that can influence a college or university's ratings and financial situation is student retention. According to the U.S. Department of Education, 42% of all college students attending college from 2000 to 2006 did not graduate. Not surprisingly, schools that are selective and choose students carefully during admissions have much better retention rates than those that do not. Better performing students tend to stay in school. Students who leave school prematurely pay less tuition, which results in financial losses to the institution, and a deterioration of institutional ratings. While a number of factors influence the economic health of colleges and universities, student tuition is one of the most important. Academic institutions rely on stable tuition to employ many people [faculty, administration, and staff] to educate the future workforce. Because colleges and universities rely so heavily on student tuition, they have high levels of concern with student quality and the behavioral outcomes of incoming and current students.

Employer Employers provide work to people and pay them for it. Employers generally are highly involved or concerned with an employee's ability to work effectively to accomplish institutional goals. Therefore, employers are likely to be very selective when it comes to hiring. Employers often formally evaluate each employee against defined goals. They may then assign individual employee ratings, record results, and communicate results to employees in performance appraisals. Results of performance appraisals influence actions such as promotions, training, salary increases, warnings, and termination. Most employers care a lot about how employee behavior contributes to the organization's success. Therefore, most employers will have high degrees of involvement with behavior.

You will have varying degrees of involvement with many other audiences: classmates, co-workers, friends, siblings, other family members, doctors, law enforcement, and so on. Regardless of whom you are communicating with, understanding what motivates and is important to each audience type will help you judge the appropriateness of your messages.

Messages

Now that we have identified some of the audiences with whom you interact and your level of involvement with each, we should now understand what messages [verbal and nonverbal] each audience is looking for from you. To determine this, we must ask the following question:

What is the single most important message that you can communicate to the various audience types that are highly involved with you?

Most people with whom you interact will want to know whether they can trust you. If people trust you, they will be more willing to associate with and help you. It is the foundation upon which long-term healthy relations with others are built. Stephen Covey writes that, "Trust is the glue of life. It's the most essential ingredient in effective communication. It's the foundational principle that holds all relationships."

What do you think?

The messages below are actual e-mails from students to professors from students. If your grade depended on it, would you confidently rely on them to represent your academic interests? Why or why not?

Message #1   "heyyyy, it [name withheld] from class i know i havent been there for a while but things have just bee crazy i went to va then go sick but il be back thur can you give me any work is missed/??"

Message #2   "hey i was wondering if you could send me the homework and everything else that we did in class and again i am sorry that i could not be there but if you would send me the homework for monday and last monday and wednesday please so that i can get what we did in class and so i can study the things and know what we did thank you that would be great thankyou see you on monday and sorry that i could not e there"

Message #3   "eye will find out, eye'm gonna have to call the library. 9-noon, thats three hours That is enough time for me to take both, right? Yeah i'm good with that.-"

_____

_____

_____

Evidence

People sift through your communications looking for behavioral evidence that you are trustworthy in all five of the trust categories. They want to see that you make good decisions regarding the people in your life, activities you're involved with, and situations that you encounter. Do you handle all of them well, or do you sometimes fall short in some way. People who do *all* of these things consistently well can be given responsibility, because they have proven that they can be trusted to handle people, activities and situations effectively. Although it is difficult to do all of these things well simultaneously, it is what behaviorally competent individuals strive to do.

How can you assess behavioral trustworthiness in people? Although it is difficult to gauge trustworthiness, there are ways. One way is to look for evidence of behavioral patterns. People with patterns of behavior often leave behind clues about the way they behave.

For example, for an individual to be deemed as considerate of others, there must be an absence of patterns of inconsiderate behavior towards others. Patterns of belittling, demeaning, or undermining others regularly would be evidence of inconsiderate behavior. If there are patterns of evidence that a person behaves in this way towards others, then the evidence would suggest that the individual is not considerate.

Another example, for an individual to be deemed capable of coping with difficult, changing, or complex situations, there should be an absence of patterns of failing to cope with these types of situations. If evidence of patterns of failure to cope emerge, then it is reasonable to infer that the individual may not cope well with similar challenging situations in the future.

Similarly, for an individual to be deemed as committed to an activity, there should be an absence of patterns of uncommitted behavior. If the evidence indicates patterns of uncommitted behavior to an activity, then it is reasonable to assume that the individual has other priorities and is not as committed to that activity. This is not to say that people cannot change their behavior. However, it does suggest that people must want to change their own behavior or it will probably continue.

Remember, communicating effectively is not easy, and the consequences of sending conflicting messages can be severe. That is why it is important to be aware of whom you are communicating with [audience], the level of concern of each audience [involvement], and what you are communicating both verbally and non-verbally [message]. When the [evidence] shows that your actions do not match your words, you erode trust. To see if you are consistently sending messages that are in your best interest, please take a few minutes to complete the following self-assessment *Communication Effectiveness: A Self-Assessment* on the next page.

Communication Effectiveness:
A Self-Assessment

Instructions: Read each of the statements below. On a scale of 1-10 (with 1 being "Never" and 10 being "Always"), circle the number that is nearest to your confidence level in how well you communicate.

1. I take time to properly construct voice, text, and e-mail communications.

   1   2   3   4   5   6   7   8   9   10

2. I understand with which of the various audience I am communicating.

   1   2   3   4   5   6   7   8   9   10

3. I understand my level of involvement with each audience type.

   1   2   3   4   5   6   7   8   9   10

4. I tailor messages to ensure that they are appropriate to the audiences with whom I communicate.

   1   2   3   4   5   6   7   8   9   10

5. I maintain a positive attitude when demands are placed on me.

   1   2   3   4   5   6   7   8   9   10

6. I communicate clearly, using appropriate style, format, grammar, and tone.

   1   2   3   4   5   6   7   8   9   10

7. I control my emotional reactions.

   1   2   3   4   5   6   7   8   9   10

8. I treat people with respect and dignity.

    1   2   3   4   5   6   7   8   9   10

9. I ask questions if I don't understand something.

    1   2   3   4   5   6   7   8   9   10

10. I listen actively by demonstrating attention to and conveying understanding of, the comments and questions of others.

    1   2   3   4   5   6   7   8   9   10

Add the numbers you circled for the ten statements.

Total Score: _____

90-100: You are a good communicator and avoid communication problems.

80-90: You are a good communicator, but you may be sending some messages that conflict with your goals.

Less than 80: Your score indicates that you are consistently sending messages that may not be in your best self-interest.

To Sum Up

Unit I focused on communication.

First, you learned how to identify the different people with whom you interact, and defined the characteristics that are unique to each type.

Second, after we identified some of the different audience types together, you learned about how you are involved with each type, and that some audience types care a great deal about your behavioral outcomes and that some might not. We also reviewed descriptions of some of the more important audience types that students and young adults communicate with.

Third, you learned what messages each audience will be looking for from you. You also learned about the importance of communicating trust.

Fourth, we discussed how your actions are evidence that substantiate claims that you make about yourself.

Lastly, you were asked to take a communication effectiveness self-assessment.

Unit 2
Choice

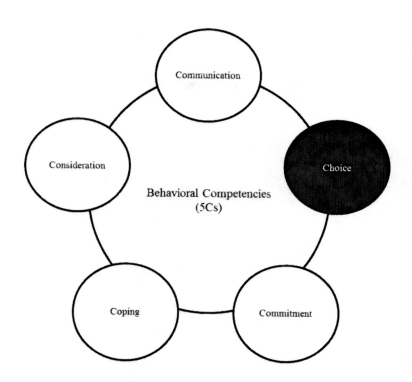

Self-Management - Understanding Behavioral Competency
Friendsville Publishing Group
Gian Paolo Roma - © 2014 - All Rights Reserved

Understanding Choice

*"Destiny is not a matter of chance; it is a matter of choice.
It is not a thing to be waited for; it is a thing to be achieved."*

~ William Jennings Bryan

At what point do people become responsible for their own actions? At what age should conscious decision-making start and acting on impulse stop? Infants are all impulse. They act and react based on the sensations in their bodies without considering consequences. They coo when they are happy and content; they cry when they are uncomfortable.

As people mature, we become aware of how our bodily sensations affect our behavior. We begin to understand cause and effect. Over time, we learn to moderate impulses based on the effect that they have on others and ourselves. We learn that impulsive behavior has consequences.

When children consciously consider something and then make a choice from different alternatives, they affect the direction of their lives. The same is true for adults. Choices are the forces that move people in one direction or another. The trajectory and outcome of each person's life is largely the result of the choices he or she has made in life. *Quick note: This text uses the terms choice and decision-making interchangeably.*

So, how do you make good choices? The ability to make good decisions is a result of proactive, careful thought and analysis of all available information relating to the matter requiring a decision. Relevant factors that should be considered prior to any decision being made are:

> (1) the role values and ethics play in decision-making
> (2) how your choices communicate your character
> (3) an *accurate* assessment or reading of current reality

These factors become the framework within which information can be gathered, organized, and analyzed when making a decision. They play an essential part in determining risk and the best course of action. Decisions made without clearly understanding these variables are more likely to produce bad results. The data is what separates sound decision-making from guesswork.

Of course, we can ignore the data and make decisions based solely on impulse. But, we should not be surprised, then, when our lives deteriorate into a uniquely worsened state that is our own doing. Although "hindsight is twenty-twenty," the formation of judgments and decisions based on inaccurate or inconclusive information and/or impulsiveness are often at the heart of most poor decision-making and regret.

Understanding Your Values and Ethics

"The only tyrant I accept in this world is the 'still small voice' within me."

~ Mohandas K. Gandhi

The choices that you make reveal your values. Values are the underlying set of principles [or rules] that govern your thinking, judgment, behavior and ultimately, every choice that you make. There are many values that inform your opinions about what is right, wrong, and just in the world. In general, decision-making that considers others and encourages the growth and development of individual dignity and respect in yourself and others is considered universally to be honorable, virtuous, and morally good. The byproduct of morally sound decision-making is trust.

In contrast, decisions that undermine individual dignity and respect result in mistrust of some kind. Keep in mind that a person can communicate trust to one audience type but not to others. Behaviorally competent people try to behave in a trustworthy manner to everyone that they encounter, not just to a select few.

Choices involve values. Ethics relate to your choice of values when you make a decision. Many situations are complex and involve more than one value. In ethics, you must choose between competing values by ranking one value over other values. Some choices are easy and some are not. Ethical decision-making forces you to select one value over other values and possibly compromise one or more values that may be very important to you. These choices can affect how you see yourself and influence the way others see you too. When the choice is difficult, you may feel "caught between a rock and a hard place." This is called an "ethical dilemma."

What choice would you make?

Would you lie under oath in a court of law to protect a friend after you saw him do something illegal?

_____

_____

_____

_____

_____

What values are important to you?

Take a few minutes and think about the people in your life. In the spaces provided below, identify the person you most admire. Why do you admire that person? After you have figured out whom you admire and why, try to identify a person that you don't admire. Why don't you admire him or her? Is your opinion of that person the result of his or her actions, deeds, or words? [If you do not feel comfortable naming names, you can just use a code word that will identify the person or people to you.]

Who is a person you admire *most*? _____

What are two personal qualities you admire most about that person?

_____

_____

Who is a person you admire *least*? _____

What are two personal qualities you dislike about that person?

_____

_____

In this exercise, we have identified together many different behavioral traits, some admirable and some not so admirable. If a person communicates that he or she is a liar, bigot, disloyal, lazy, unreliable, mean, or abusive, he or she can become defined by those behavioral qualities. By contrast, those who are consistently honest, loyal, fair-minded, hard-working, reliable, and respectful of others, tend to be trusted and respected by others. You expected these people to behave in certain ways. One person lived up to your expectations and the other did not.

Just as you expect others to behave in certain ways, others will have expectations of you. They will be looking for behavioral evidence that they can confidently rely on you. People will be more apt to help and support you if they admire and trust you. Years from now, if your family, friends, and associates are asked whom they most admire and least admire, what list will you be on? If you believe that you will be on the "admired" list, what behavioral evidence can you provide to substantiate your belief?

Understanding Your Character

"I must first know myself ...
to be curious about that which is not my concern,
while I am still in ignorance of my own self would be ridiculous."

~ Plato

As discussed earlier, your words and actions communicate facts and information about yourself that influence how others see you. Your choices communicate what is distinctive about you. Your choices continually transmit information about your values, ethics, judgment, manner, emotions, friendliness, interest, desire, motivation, attitude, aptitude, dependability, and work ethic. In short, your choices reveal your character and true nature.

How you are perceived is largely a consequence of your behavioral choices. In life, the choices you make about how you say and do things, how hard you work, how nice you are to others, how dependable you are, how you deal with your problems, etc. are all plain and clear for others to see, understand, and interpret. As such, your choices define you to others. Not only that, your own self-image will be shaped in part by those very same choices.

Making decisions that are good for you begins with an understanding of the type of person you want to be. If you want to be a trustworthy person, then your choices should be worthy of trust. For example, if you don't show up to your classes, your poor attendance will characterize you to your professors as being less committed than those that show up. Showing up to class is a *choice of action* that others will use to describe the type of person that they see and/or experience.

The type of person you want to be is a destination or endpoint toward which your judgment and choices should take you. In the same way that you cannot chart a course to an unknown destination, you cannot make the best choices for yourself if you do not know the type of person that you want to be. Do you understand the behavioral traits that define your character?

What type of person do you want to be?

Try to imagine that all of your high school teachers had a meeting about you and that you could eavesdrop on that meeting. What would you *hope* the teachers would say about you? On the next page is a list of personal qualities. Please list [in order of importance] the top five personal qualities that you would *hope* your teachers would say about you. What you *hope* they would say may not be the same as what they would actually say. Only list the personal qualities that you hope that they would say about you that would bring you the most amount of joy. If the words below are not descriptive enough for you, please list other words that you would hope others would use to describe you.

Self-Management - Understanding Behavioral Competency
Friendsville Publishing Group
Gian Paolo Roma - © 2014 - All Rights Reserved

1. Considerate	13. Accountable	25. Strong	37. Cooperative
2. Interested	14. Forgiving	26. Stable	38. Stamina
3. Hard working	15. Honorable	27. Survivor	39. Ambitious
4. Pursues excellence	16. Kind	28. Energetic	40. Determined
5. Open minded	17. Committed	29. Charismatic	41. Trustworthy
6. Honest	18. Competent	30. Responsible	42. Punctual
7. Courageous	19. Happy	31. Motivated	43. Competitive
8. Modest	20. Graceful	32. Dignified	44. Humble
9. Safety conscious	21. Adaptable	33. Prepared	45. Helpful
10. Objective	22. Status conscious	34. Empathic	46. Loyal
11. Reliable	23. Fair minded	35. Excitable	47. Sincere
12. Secure	24. Friendly	36. Passionate	48. Cool

1. _____

2. _____

3. _____

4. _____

5. _____

Character Statement

Next, using just one sentence, starting with "I would hope they would say that I was …", please write down your character statement or personal policy that you would like to guide your behavioral conduct and decision-making going forward. QUICK TIP: What would you like your friends, family and colleagues to say about you at your funeral? What would make you feel content?

I would hope they would say that I was … _____

_____

_____

It is never too late to become the person that you want to be. How you choose to interact with the rest of the world is up to you. Your own daily choices will determine your character and the type of person you become. Choose wisely because choices communicate your character to others.

Understanding Your Reality

"We cannot change the cards we are dealt, just how we play the hand."

~ Randy Pausch

As we talked about at the beginning of this unit, the outcome of each person's life will be largely the result of the choices he or she has made. If one considers the type of person he or she wants to be as the *end-point* of our decision-making, one must next define accurately his or her *start-point,* to figure out how he or she is going to become that person. For example, if a pilot wants to fly to Los Angeles, the best route to get there depends on where the pilot starts. The directions to Los Angeles are completely different from New York than they are from Miami. In order for you to reach your desired *end-point*, you must know your start-point, from which your decision-making must always begin.

Other factors such as safety, weather, engine, and air traffic problems may also influence pilot decision-making along the way to the end-point or destination. For example, pilots can change course to avoid severe turbulence if they know beforehand about severe weather conditions. The line between the two points may be straight or meandering depending on what is encountered along the way. By understanding as much as we can about the nature and meaning of our start-point or current reality *before* we make decisions, we can anticipate opportunities and problems before they happen and make changes or adjustments along the way to our end-point. How you get to your end-point is your choice. Try to remember that decision-making without accurate information about your current situation is nothing more than guesswork. It is like a flying plane on a foggy night without instrument gauges, or *"flying blind."*

Seeing your current reality clearly is much like seeing the picture on the box of a jigsaw puzzle emerge with the assembly of each puzzle piece. You try to put together as many small, interlocking pieces of information as you can. Each piece of information has on it a small part of the picture about your current reality. The more pieces of reality that you put together, the clearer the picture of your current reality will become.

Unlike jigsaw puzzles however, decisions are usually made without having a complete picture of the reality of a situation. The goal is to assemble enough information to make your current reality as clear as possible before the decision. If information arrives after a decision has been made, it cannot inform the decision. Therefore, good decision-making requires information be timely. If the information is timely, then the next requirement for good decision-making is good information.

Good choices depend on good information. Choices are only as good as the information that informs them. If information is bad, the resulting decision will probably be bad, unless luck intervenes. It is a good idea to verify the accuracy of the information supplied whenever you are making a decision. This is true especially when decisions are critical or when the information source is unreliable. Bad information begets bad choices. Or as Sophocles said, "No enemy is worse than bad advice."

If the information is both timely and good, then the last requirement for making good decisions is to make sure that you have as much information as needed to make the decision. Making decisions without having enough information is called conclusion jumping, and can be just as error-prone as decisions made with bad information. The saying is "on your mark, get set, go," not "on your mark, go, get set."

At what point can you feel comfortable making decisions? If you can begin to see how the decision will affect your reality one day, one week, one month, one year, or five years out, then you increase the probability that the outcome of your decision-making will be as you predicted. If you cannot begin to see how the decision will affect your future reality, then you are probably *"conclusion-jumping"* and need to gather more information.

Appendices

Located at the back of the book are two appendices that have been designed to help you gather information about college and about yourself. Specifically, in Appendix I, you will find the current U.S. Department of Labor data about the effect that a college education has on career earnings and employment. By gathering this real-world data, you will be better able to see for yourself the value of graduating from college.

In Appendix II you will gather information about the external realities [opportunities and threats] influencing your world today. In addition, you will define your own unique internal realities [strengths and weaknesses] that exist within you. By understanding your internal and external realities, you will be in a better position to judge the appropriateness of your decision-making.

	Page		Title
Appendix I	95		Effect of Educational Attainment on Career Earnings and Employment
Appendix II	101		Reality Assessment

To Sum Up

Unit 2 focused on choices.

First, we learned that our choices communicate judgment-based trust.

Second, you learned that the choices people make define their character and those choices have consequences. You learned that good information is required to make good choices.

Third, making good choices is a function of three variables: understanding your own values and ethics, understanding the type of person that you'd like to be, and accurately identifying your situation at the time of the decision. These three variables provide the framework and information within which decision-making occurs. The overall goal is to gather enough information about these three variables to feel comfortable estimating the consequences of the decision under consideration.

Fourth, in the assignments at the end of the book, you learned about the effect education has on career earnings and employment and how to perform a "Reality Assessment." You defined in groups some of the macro External Reality [opportunities and threats] influencing the world today. In addition, you defined your own unique set of Internal Reality [strengths and weaknesses] that exist within you. You were then asked to write down how you might be able to align your internal strengths with the external opportunities you identified. Lastly, you were asked to think about how you might go about improving some of the internal weakness you identified.

Unit 3
Commitment

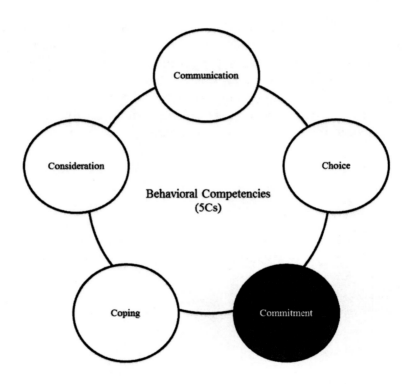

Self-Management - Understanding Behavioral Competency
Friendsville Publishing Group
Gian Paolo Roma - © 2014 - All Rights Reserved

Understanding Commitment

"Commitment is an act, not a word."

~ Jean Paul Sartre

Our behaviors communicate traits about the way we function, and those traits affect how others see us and how we see ourselves. Character traits are distinguishing features of an individual's nature. These traits create lasting impressions in the minds of people who experience our behavior. One of the most important character traits an individual can communicate is commitment. Commitment is a trait that communicates an individual's ...

willingness to expend time and energy, at the exclusion of other activities, to meet his or her obligations to others.

Commitment is an emotional and intellectual devotion to one activity over other activities. In general, if an individual is committed to an activity, he or she gives that activity more attention and time than to other activities. The activity is treated as a priority and is moved to the "front burner" to meet its requirements. As Jean Paul Sartre explains in the above quote, commitment is an act and as such is communicated non-verbally. Words cannot do homework, show up to class, hammer a nail, build a bridge, play a violin concerto, or put a person on the moon. Only activity [actions and deeds] can do these things.

We can think intellectually about commitment related behaviors as either *strengthening* or *weakening* trust, or *"productive"* or *"unproductive"* respectively. *Productive* behaviors such as showing up on time, working hard, and producing high-quality output, strengthen trust connections with the audiences that experience the behavior. While *unproductive* behaviors such as lack of effort, being unreliable, poor quality output, and lack of accountability can weaken goodwill and cooperation, and may require other people to step in to encourage more trustworthy performance.

There are three commitment variables that can be measured and analyzed to determine an individual's level of commitment to an activity. Figure 3-1 on the next page shows the three variables that demonstrate commitment: dependability, hard work, and work quality[5].

---

[5] Adapted from Kathryn Jackson's writings from two articles:

 i. Response Design Corporation, Kathryn Jackson, "How to Set Performance Standards to Ensure Excellent Service", Product No. 10038, http://www.responsedesign.com/store/10038.pdf, also

 ii. Response Design Corporation, Kathryn Jackson, "Adapting Schedule Adherence Measurement to Improve Performance", Product No. 10038, http://www.responsedesign.com/store/10039.pdf

Commitment Model

Figure 3.1

The Venn diagram demonstrates the overlapping relationship between the three commitment variables, which means that certain behaviors can affect all of the variables simultaneously. For instance, dependability related issues, like not showing up to class, could reveal problems with student work ethic, and at the same time, be the cause of poor academic quality.

These three variables are evidence of behavioral commitment. Skill, with few exceptions, is learned and a direct result of these three variables. In the same way that playing the violin is a learned skill, so too is reading, writing, language, mathematics, music, nursing, accounting, surgery, litigation, plumbing, masonry, carpentry, cutting hair, writing computer code, stand up comedy, basketball, chemistry, and so on. And just as one cannot expect to play the violin at Carnegie Hall without commitment, one cannot expect to have acquired skill at any activity [academic, career, personal, or social] without commitment. High levels of skill suggest high levels of commitment, while low levels of skill imply low levels of commitment.

Let's take a look at the three commitment variables in more detail.

Understanding Dependability

"People count up the faults of those who keep them waiting."

~ French Proverb

The first behavioral variable that communicates commitment [an individual's willingness to expend time and energy, at the exclusion of other activities, to meet obligations to others] is dependability. As shown in the Dependability Model below [Figure 3.2], dependability is a function of three behavioral components: [1] showing up on time; [2] being prepared; [3] and being ready to perform the required duties. Words cannot do these three things.

Dependability Model

Figure 3.2

If any of the variables on the left-hand side of the equation are low, the result or product [dependability] on the right-hand side will also be low. For example, if a construction worker consistently shows up to work on time and is also prepared with the proper tools, but *not* ready to perform his or her duties responsibly because he or she is sleep-deprived or hung-over, he or she may not be viewed as being dependable. In academia, some students consistently show up to class on time, but are not prepared because their homework is not complete. These students communicate to the instructor that they are less dependable and committed to the class than students who show up on time with completed homework.

A high level of dependability inspires confidence in people, while a low level of dependability has the exact opposite effect. Individuals who do not faithfully show up on time, prepared, and ready to perform their duties communicate an unwillingness to meet their obligations to others. In short, they "deprioritize" these obligations, and in doing so, communicate that they cannot be confidently relied on to perform their duties consistently.

Audiences [e.g. supervisors, professors, advisors, parents, etc.] that are responsible for the success or failure of activities may conclude rightfully that undependable people cannot be trusted to meet their obligations to them. The behavior creates doubt in the minds of the people that experience it, which may cause them to act in a manner that safeguards their own interests. Also, it doesn't really matter how smart or capable an undependable person is, the behavior will create doubt that undermines trust.

Undependable people prioritize their own desires ahead of the interests, needs, and wishes of others. The behavior communicates *nonverbally* that the personal needs and wishes of the undependable person are more important than those of others. Try to keep that in mind as you make choices during your day. Even the most casual decisions, like choosing to sleep in instead of consistently showing up, being on time, or being ready to perform, can weaken your credibility and possibly even sever the trust that binds you to those people.

In addition to trust, there are other reasons why dependability is critically important. People who are committed to showing up on time, prepared, and being ready to do what is required of them, are more safe, more successful, less expensive to keep around, and better team members than people who do not dependably act in this manner.

Let's take a look at each of these byproducts of dependability.

Dependability and Safety

The first and probably most serious reason that dependability matters is safety. In some occupations, *not* consistently showing up, being late, or not being ready to perform one's duties can actually endanger the health and welfare of coworkers. Firefighters, police officers, and members of the armed forces, all must confidently rely on the dependability of their coworkers when they go to work. They trust that their coworkers will be dependable and it would be a major ethical breach to do otherwise. If firefighters, police officers, or members of the armed forces are not dependable, they could seriously compromise the safety of everyone on their team.

Also, doctors, lawyers, nurses, paramedics, Red Cross workers, road crews, security guards, air traffic controllers, crossing guards, pilots, etc. must be dependable or they could compromise the safety of the public that depends on them. Below is an example of how quickly a situation can spiral out of control when an individual on a team is not dependable. The story is a personal account of what can happen when a co-worker is not dependable.

> When I was a patrol officer, there was another police officer who had recently been hired and who had a reputation for not being dependable. On one occasion, I was dispatched to a bar fight. Serious injuries had already occurred. "Joe" was my backup officer. I arrived at the bar fight first. Unfortunately, the bar fight had spilled out into the parking lot, so I could not wait for my backup to arrive. As I got out of my car, I heard the dispatcher continuing to call "Joe", but he did not respond. I continued anyway and in the process of breaking up the fight, I got hit a few times and stabbed. Not until I got everything under control did Joe show up. As it turned out, Joe was busy away from his car socializing with a woman. The dispatcher finally got him on the radio and he "ran code" all the way to the bar fight. But, it was too late. I made the arrests, stopped the fight, and made my way to the emergency room. "Joe' though he arrived while I was still on scene, made his way to a reputation as unreliable and undependable. [6]

What dependability variables or rules did Joe violate? Explain.

_____

_____

_____

_____

---

[6] Personal story of Greg Talley former Associate VP, Dean, and Professor at SUNY Broome Community College and Chief of Police in Los Alamos, New Mexico

Dependability and Success

The second reason why dependability is important is that it affects success. Being dependable influences one's success as a student and an employee. To try to understand how student dependability impacts academic success, I gathered attendance and grade data for all of the 206 students that completed my Accounting I, Accounting II and Human Resources Management courses over a 17-month period. The study only included students that received a final grade, and did *not* include students that withdrew before a final grade could be given. To gather the attendance data, I had students sign an attendance log at the beginning of every class. Table 3.1 below summarizes the findings of the study.

Table 3.1

Attendance	Number of Students	% of Total	GPA	Average Grade
0 Classes missed	47	22.8%	3.3	B+
1-4 classes missed classes	96	46.6%	2.8	B-
5-8 classes missed classes	32	15.5%	2.2	C
More than 8 missed classes	32	15.5%	1.2	D
Totals	206			

Note: Attendance is not factored into my grading.

As the numbers show, there is a substantial correlation between final GPA and class attendance. Students with fewer absences received higher grades, while students with lower grades had higher absenteeism. As a matter of fact, students that did not miss any classes had 15% and 33% higher grades than students that missed 1-4 classes or 5-8 classes respectively.

The findings make sense because going to class is one of the primary ways that students acquire knowledge about the subjects they take. The other ways are of course reading textbooks, solving problems, doing homework, writing research papers, etc. But class is where professors introduce subject matter material, answer questions, assign and explain homework, review for tests, and discuss their expectations. Students that attended class consistently were better prepared for the tests. The more prepared students answered more test questions correctly.

Lastly, 11.2% of the students in this study received failing grades, and *none* of the students with perfect attendance failed.

Dependability and Cost

In an employment setting, undependable people are expensive to keep around. Prior to teaching, I was as a member of a wireless start-up company that is now part of T-Mobile, USA. My last position at the company was in customer service senior management. My department was responsible for, among other things, scheduling a 1000+ person workforce at two 24/7 customer contact centers.

One of the most important variables we tracked in the department was how well customer contact representatives adhered to the schedules that we had given them. We tracked electronically when representatives were logged into the systems to take calls, how long they were logged into the systems, and how long they were logged out. Our goal was to achieve 90% schedule adherence. Which meant that for an eight-hour shift, with 30 minutes for lunch and two 15-minute breaks, representatives should have been logged into the systems for 378 minutes each day. Our goal was to have all of our 1000 representatives logged into the systems, ready to take calls for a total of [1000 representatives x 378 minutes = *378,000 minutes*] each day.

What we found out was that our representatives were only adhering to their daily schedules 80% of the time, not the 90% that we had budgeted for. This meant that all 1000 representatives were actually logged into our system ready to take calls for an average of only 336,000 minutes instead of the scheduled 378,000 minutes. The *42,000* minute difference in performance between scheduled to actual meant that the company was paying for the equivalent of about *100 full-time equivalent employees* to show up and *not* work. If the average representative costs approximately $35,000 fully loaded cost [salary, benefits, etc] per year, the cost to the company of operating at 80% schedule adherence is [$35,000 x 100 representatives = *$3,500,000* per year.

What are some ways the company might address the dependability problem among its workers?

_____

_____

_____

_____

_____

_____

Dependability and Teamwork

Being undependable creates a lot more work for everyone else on a team. The work for firefighters, police officers, sales people, waitresses, construction workers, call center representatives, maintenance workers, dentists, manufacturing workers, etc. does not go away when people don't show up, or are late, unprepared, or not ready to perform duties. The work is moved or shifted to everyone else on a work team who is dependable.

Imagine the following scenario. It's a hot and humid summer afternoon and you are the owner of an ice cream shop. There is a continuous line throughout the day of about 300 customers, but only two of three workers you had scheduled to work show up. The worker that did not come to work was a "no call, no show." Instead of servicing 300 customers between a team of three workers, you must now service all 300 customers between a team of only two. Without the third worker, customers would wait longer for service, and some might get frustrated and leave the store, which would increase stress and frustration for the entire work team and hurt business.

What opinion would you have of an undependable person who increased your workload?

_____

_____

_____

Think about it

I once had an employee who would call in sick from time to time. When we pulled his attendance log, which shows what days he missed for an entire year on one sheet of paper, we noticed that every few weeks he got sick on either Monday or Friday. What does the pattern tell you? Quick note: Many students also demonstrate this exact same dependability pattern in college.

_____

_____

_____

Dependability Effectiveness:
A Self-Assessment

Take a couple of minutes to rate the dependability statements below.

Instructions: Read each of the statements below. On a scale of 1-10 (with 1 being "Never" and 10 being "Always"), circle the number that is nearest to your confidence level in making the transition to college.

1. I have the textbooks and all supplies required for my classes.

   1   2   3   4   5   6   7   8   9   10

2. I attend and am on time for my classes.

   1   2   3   4   5   6   7   8   9   10

3. I am alert and ready to learn when I am in class.

   1   2   3   4   5   6   7   8   9   10

4. I complete assigned homework prior to class.

   1   2   3   4   5   6   7   8   9   10

5. I prepare for exams.

   1   2   3   4   5   6   7   8   9   10

Add the numbers you circled for the five statements.

Total Score: _____

45-50: Your score indicates that you are aware of and concerned about being dependable.

40-44: You score indicates that you are only dependable 80%-88% of the time, which may be impacting your grades.

Less than 40: Your score indicates that your lack of dependability is probably impacting your grades.

Self-Management - Understanding Behavioral Competency
Friendsville Publishing Group
Gian Paolo Roma - © 2014 - All Rights Reserved

Dependability Personal Policy

Please take a few minutes to think about and write down your personal policy commitments regarding [1] showing up to class on time, [2] being prepared, and [3] being ready to perform? Please write down what you will commit to in the spaces provided below.

Dependability Variable	Commitment Statement
[1] showing up to class on time	[1] example: I will commit to leaving 15 minutes earlier than I do so that I will not be late to class.
[2] being prepared	[2] example: I will commit to completing all of my homework assignments before I go to class.
[3] being ready to perform	[3] example: I will never show up to class without my textbook

Understanding Hard Work

"Nothing ever comes to one that is worth having except as a result of hard work."

~ *Booker T. Washington*

The second element of commitment is hard work. In tough economic times, it is easy to think that success comes only to those who are lucky or advantaged in some way. Although it may be true that luck and connections play a role in success, an overwhelming body of evidence shows that success is more the result of hard work[7]. Hard work puts people in a position to be lucky. Or as Thomas Jefferson once said, "I'm a great believer in luck, and I find the harder I work, the more I have of it."

If hard work is so important to skill development, why do some people avoid working hard? I think the answer may be that they may not understand fully how hard they are working relative to everyone else. Some people may think they are working hard, when in fact they may not be.

How hard you are working depends on whom you compare yourself with. If you compare yourself against students that only spend three hours studying for an exam and you study nine hours, then you may view yourself as being a hard worker. But if other students were studying for 27 hours, then they would be working three times harder than you.

It is difficult to see what other students are doing. In today's global economy, you can no longer compare yourself to only the people in your classroom. You are competing with people from around the world. It takes a lot of hard work to understand advanced mathematics, physics, or chemistry especially when the answers are not intuitively obvious. It takes hard work to become a nurse, accountant, actor, computer programmer, tennis player etc. However, a strong work ethic is exactly what you need to develop skills that are required to compete effectively in this global economy.

Think of it as developing survival skills. One-thousand years ago parents taught their children survival skills, such as how to hunt, farm, live off the land, make clothing, and provide shelter. If parents did not hunt, their families starved. If they did not make clothing or provide shelter, their families might die of exposure to the elements. Their children were taught these skills so that they could survive and prosper.

Today, *you* need to learn survival skills. Although the technical skills are much different than 1,000 years ago, behavioral skills [like working hard and being dependable] are essentially unchanged. Hard work is challenging intellectually, emotionally, and physically. Hard work is not easy. If it were, it would be called play.

---

[7] John A. Sloboda, Jane W. Davidson, Michael J. A. Howe, Derek G. Moore, "The role of practice in the development of performing musicians", *British Journal of Psychology*, Volume 87, Issue 2, pages 287–309, May 1996

Hard work has three defining characteristics: time and deliberate practice, delayed gratification, and effort. As shown in the Hard Work Model below [Figure 3.3], the product of these variables equals the value of your work output.

Hard Work Model

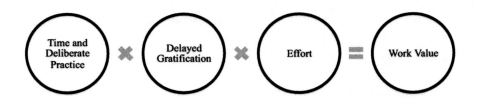

Figure 3.3

Although some students work very hard, others do not appear to make the connection between hard work and the value of their knowledge, skills, and abilities [KSAs]. Today, employers are increasingly looking for employees that can use their KSAs to make organizations more efficient, effective, and competitive. They are searching domestically and internationally for people with highly developed KSAs that add value. They are not looking for employees with skill in understanding the obvious.

For a variety of reasons that are beyond the scope of this book, many of the low- and medium-skill jobs that once paid well and characterized America's economy have slowly been either automated or outsourced. Consequently, to acquire the higher-level KSAs required for today's competitive world, students must be willing to put in time, practice deliberately, delay gratification, and expend effort. It is that simple. There are no short cuts to real skill development.

Time

"Don't say you don't have enough time. You have exactly the same number of hours per day that were given to Helen Keller, Pasteur, Michelangelo, Mother Teresa, Leonardo da Vinci, Thomas Jefferson, and Albert Einstein."

~ Life's Little Instruction Book

Time gives us the ability to see the consequences of our actions on our lives. One cannot become a first-rate doctor, musician, nurse, lawyer, writer, salesperson, computer programmer, mechanical engineer, artist, etc. without investing large amounts of time developing those skill sets.

According to researchers, time is a primary ingredient to developing skills.[8] They estimate that it takes about 10 years of practice [two to three hours per day] to develop world-class expertise in any field. That's about 10,000 hours. [The only exception to this rule is height, body mass, and quickness]. Their research sites a 1994 study that found that exceptional talent in music, mathematics, chess or sports "required lengthy periods of instruction and practice."[9] The most exceptionally talented students put in a lot more time than did less talented students. Their research found also that it did not matter how "talented" the musicians were when they started. None of the elite performers were "naturals" who did not put in long hours of practice. The most talented people were not always naturally gifted when they started, or the smartest; they were the people who put in the most time and practice. The research gives new meaning to the phrase; "Hard work beats talent, when talent doesn't work hard."

This same concept also applies to academics. If you put enough time into your studies, you will develop academic skill. It takes time to learn how to read and write well. It takes time to become proficient in mathematics or a language. Although it helps to have great teachers, your own commitment to succeed may be far more important than any other factor. Genuine skill development requires a real sacrifice of time, not just 15 minutes here or 15 minutes there doing homework, while texting, or on Facebook or Instagram.

How you spend your time is a key part of demonstrating that you work hard.

---

[8] Anders K. Ericsson, Ralf T Krampe, Clemens Tesch-Römer,; "The role of deliberate practice in the acquisition of expert performance", *Psychological Review*, Vol 100(3), Jul 1993, 363-406.

[9] ibid

Deliberate Practice

"For the things we have to learn before we can do them, we learn by doing them."
~ Aristotle

Working hard is particularly difficult when you lack the skills or ability to do it well. Practicing something that you are not proficient at requires much more concentration than practicing something that you excel at.[10] In the article, "The Making of an Expert", researchers point out that "Deliberate practice entails considerable, specific and sustained effort to do something you *can't* do well. It involves improving the skills you already have and extending the reach and range of your skills."[11] For example, the best basketball players in the world can shoot and dribble with their right and their left hand. They can shoot the ball moving to the left and the right. They methodically and repeatedly practice every aspect of the game day after day, week after week, month after month, and year after year. They don't just play pick-up ball with friends. They develop world-class basketball skills by systematically thinking through and practicing what they are good at, as well as what they are *not* good at. They continually work to improve *every* aspect of their game. Practice does not make perfect. Deliberate practice makes perfect.

Because deliberate practice requires much more concentration, it is hard to do for long periods of time. One can only devote "a couple hours a day"[12] to deliberate practice because it requires so much focus. Nevertheless, people who are deliberate in their approach to skill development and hard work, practice a couple of hours every day for years. It all adds up. For example, if you practice writing every day for a couple of hours, you will total almost three thousand hours in just four years. Three thousand hours is enough time to become a good writer.

College is all about learning new subject matter. Some subjects you may be good at, and some you may not. Some classes are more demanding than others. Sitting and staring at subject matter that you find difficult for hours on end is not productive. A better way is to concentrate for smaller amounts of time in a deliberate way. For some subjects involving problem solving, such as math, accounting, economics, or physics, the key is to know how to approach the problems. For students who are having difficulty with these types of classes, it may not be possible to do the work without a basic understanding of the logic and how the formulas work. To gain that understanding, deliberate practice might involve working with a tutor for a few hours every week to practice the formulas. After gaining a basic understanding of how to solve problems, deliberate practice might then involve doing problems repeatedly [a couple hours at a time] to reinforce the learning.

---

[10] See the entire article K. Anders Ericsson, Michael J. Prietula, Edward T. Cokely, "The Making of an Expert", *Harvard Business Review*, July/August 2007
[11] ibid
[12] ibid

For courses that emphasize writing, whether essays, short stories, or research papers, basic writing skills will be required. A brilliant idea that is not written well will undermine the quality of anyone's work. If a student lacks the basic writing skills required for these courses, deliberate practice might involve working at a writing lab for an hour or two each day to learn how to approach writing assignments and how to write. Deliberate practice is not just spending four hours to produce a poorly written paper.

Because deliberate practice involves doing things that you are not good at, you will be doing things that make you feel uncomfortable, frustrated, or even scared. These feelings are natural. Anytime you do something outside of your comfort zone, you might feel unsure of yourself. In order to develop the skills you need and accomplish your goals, you must try as hard as you can to push yourself forward and cope with those feelings.

What are the areas of academic study in which you do not do well and need to improve? Does deliberate practice influence the way you will approach your studies?

Time Worksheet
A Self-Assessment

Developing the ability to do something well requires a lot of time. As you have seen, time is one of the most important ingredients in developing skills of any kind. To help understand how you use your time, please fill out the following worksheet. After calculating the time you spend on each activity, add the times together and they should come close to 168 hours, the total number of hours/week.

ITEM	ACTIVITY	TIME
1.	Sleeping	
2.	School	
3.	Employment	
4.	Domestic [parenting, cooking, cleaning, shopping, dishes]	
5.	Leisure	
6.	Commuting	
7.	Exercising	
8.	Religious observance, volunteer work	
9.	Procrastination	
10.	Studying	
11.	Other	
	TOTAL HOURS PER WEEK	168

Do you feel that have enough time to do everything you need to accomplish your academic goals? If not, what could you give up, or spend less time doing to free up more time? Can you eliminate any obvious time-wasters to increase the amount of time you devote to your schoolwork? Try to remember not to prioritize unimportant matters in front of important matters.

_____

_____

_____

_____

Self-Management - Understanding Behavioral Competency
Friendsville Publishing Group
Gian Paolo Roma - © 2014 - All Rights Reserved

Time
Action Plan

Please list the top time wasters that you have identified. Then think about and write in the space provided the actions you need to take to allocate your time more wisely.

Time Item(s) of Concern

Item 1	
Item 2	
Item 3	
Item 4	

Time Actions Required

Item	*Time Action Plan*	*Date Required*

Delayed Gratification

"You cannot escape the responsibility of tomorrow by evading it today."

~ Abraham Lincoln

Another important element of hard work is the ability to delay gratification. Delaying gratification involves postponing more pleasurable or enjoyable activities until after your work is completed. Why is delaying gratification important? According to Stanford University researchers, people who are *unable* to delay gratification, "have more behavioral problems, in school and at home," than people who have developed this ability. Problems of "low-delaying adults" cited in the research include lower SAT scores, trouble paying attention, difficulty with friendships, higher body-mass index, and problems with drugs and alcohol.[13]

High-delaying students tend to deal with their problems head on and do so immediately. Low-delaying students are more likely to procrastinate, which only makes their problems worse. Instead of doing their work right away, they may put off their work, which only serves to magnify their tension and stress. The amount of work that needs to be done in a shorter period of time may become insurmountable. New and conceptually difficult subject matter requires a great deal of concentration, which limits the quantity of material one can learn each day. For example, if it takes forty hours of deliberate practice to learn fully all of the material for a Calculus exam, it is almost impossible to learn that amount of material in one or two nights.

The human brain functions in much the same way as the human stomach. You cannot starve yourself for three weeks and then eat three weeks worth of meals in one or two nights. Your stomach would not be able to digest so much food that quickly. The same is true for your brain. No matter how hard you try, your brain cannot concentrate on conceptually difficult work like writing or complex math for more than two or three hours in a day before shutting down.[14] Also, it is doubly hard to focus when you are feeling stressed because you have to prepare for a test.

Multitasking is one of the ways students procrastinate doing their work. A Kaiser Family study found that many young people are spending a huge amount of time multitasking with media.[15] In 1999, total multitasking time by young people using media [time spent with TV, music,

---

[13] Harriet Nerlove Mischel, Walter Mischel, The Development of Children's Knowledge of Self-Control Strategies, Stanford University, *Society for Research in Child Development, Inc*, 1983

[14] John A. Sloboda, Jane W. Davidson, Michael J. A. Howe, Derek G. Moore, "The role of practice in the development of performing musicians", British Journal of Psychology, Volume 87, Issue 2, pages 287–309, May 1996

[15] Victoria J. Rideout, M.A., Ulla G. Foehr, Ph.D., Donald F. Roberts, Ph.D., "Generation M2: Media In the Lives of 8- to 18-year-olds", *A Kaiser Family Foundation Study*, January 2010, p.2

computer, video games, print, movies], averaged 6 hours and 19 minutes per day. By 2009, total multitasking media time increased more than 1 hour and 19 minutes to an average of 7 hours and 38 minutes per day, a 19 percent increase. The 1999 number was bad enough, but the 2009 number is even more troubling. Increasingly, young people are spending more and more time on the internet, playing video games, watching television, or texting, instead of developing the skills that they will need to compete in today's global economy. As an aside, the Kaiser study also found that over the same period, time spent reading decreased from 43 to 38 minutes. Why is multi-tasking so problematic?

As noted previously, activities that require a high degree of comprehension [such as writing research papers, studying for exams, doing homework, etc.] do not lend themselves well to multitasking [handling more than one task at the same time]. Activity comprehension demands concentration and that we focus _all_ of our attention on that activity.

Texting while driving is a good example. Driving requires that you have "real-time" knowledge of what is happening on the road. Texting moves your attention away from controlling a motor vehicle to reading and typing words into a cell phone. Once attention is distracted, your ability to comprehend and react to what is happening on the road diminishes. The National Safety Council describes distracted driving as "any non-driving activity a person engages in that has the potential to distract a driver from the primary task of driving and increase the risk of crashing." [16]

Because multitasking involves more than one activity, it requires some level of distraction from the primary activity. Multi-tasking, by definition, is distracted activity. The main problem with distracted activity in learning is that it reduces one's ability to concentrate, thus reducing comprehension. Three main types of distraction impact learning[17]:

1. Visual—taking your eyes off the learning material [reading, writing, lecturer, etc.]
2. Manual—taking your hands off the learning material [book, pencil, computer, etc.]
3. Cognitive—taking your mind off the learning material

As you probably already know, procrastination is a hard habit to break. Delaying gratification is how hard working people avoid procrastination. They get their work done before they take part in leisure activities like going out, communicating with friends via Instagram, Twitter, Facebook, texting, playing video games, watching TV, and web surfing. By delaying these activities until after their work is done, they can more fully enjoy their leisure time.

---

[16] Indiana Criminal Justice Institute, "*Distracted Driving*", http:// http://www.in.gov/cji/3553.htm

[17] Ibid [List from distracted driving wording copy on http:// http://www.in.gov/cji/3553.htm]

Think about it.

While all distractions reduce learning comprehension to some degree, some are more harmful to learning because they involve all three types of distractions. Can you think of activities that you do while studying that distract you visually, manually, and cognitively?

_____

_____

_____

_____

_____

_____

Please watch a TED video of speaker Joachim de Posada: "Don't eat the marshmallow!" http://www.ted.com/talks/joachim_de_posada_says_don_t_eat_the_marshmallow_yet.html? Are you a marshmallow eater [Yes or No]? If yes, please explain.

_____

_____

_____

_____

_____

_____

_____

Effort

"Footprints on the sands of time are not made by sitting down."

~ Unknown Author

More than 2400 years ago Sophocles said, "Success is dependent on effort." This is still true today. It is through effort that difficult tasks are accomplished. The more difficult the work, the more effort one must expend. For example, demanding mental activities, such as writing and math, may require much more concentration and focus than less demanding activities.[18] Effort is the outward physical manifestation of hard work, and as such, it is what people see and hear. We communicate our willingness to expend effort in many ways.

In my sophomore year in college, I got a C in a course called "Marriage and the Family." Upon hearing the news of my poor grade, my father said, "I see you got a C in marriage and the family, how did this happen?" I came up with some excuse and tried to blame the teacher." He stopped me and said, "N*obody* gets Cs in Marriage and the Family." After a brief back and forth, he said simply that he was no longer going to help pay for my education. And that was that. He saw that I was not willing to expend even a minimum of effort to get a respectable grade in what he considered an easy course.

The lesson here is that your level of effort is visible to others. People that do not work hard may be considered by others to be lazy or undisciplined. Keep this in mind when you see people that don't show up to class or are unprepared.

Think about it.

What does a student's grade point average communicate? Explain your answer.

_____

_____

_____

_____

_____

---

[18] Anders K. Ericsson, Ralf T Krampe, Clemens Tesch-Römer,; "The role of deliberate practice in the acquisition of expert performance", *Psychological Review*, Vol 100(3), Jul 1993, 363-406.

Effort has three defining characteristics: energy, determination, and stamina.

Energy

Energy relates to the intensity of your resolve to accomplish work. If your energy level is high, your resolve to work hard is high, and vice versa. A consistently high energy level communicates a high tolerance for work, or desire to work hard. While a consistently low energy level communicates a lack of concern or lack of initiative to work hard. Although many things can affect your energy level in college, [e.g. the difficulty of the work, interest in the subject-matter, etc.] energy is simply a measure of the enthusiasm you bring to your schoolwork.

On a 1-10 scale, [with "1 being little or no energy and 10 being the most energy] how much energy do you expend to complete your homework and study for tests? What are the factors you considered in coming up with your rating?

_____

_____

_____

Determination

Determination concerns the firmness of your resolve to complete work, especially when conditions become uncertain or difficult. Subjects that you find conceptually difficult or boring, perhaps organic chemistry, calculus, literature, or corporate finance, may test your level of determination. Highly determined students will hang in there when the going gets tough. They persevere despite obstacles and setbacks. As the saying goes, "When the going gets tough, the tough get going." Less determined students might give up, withdraw, or even drop out of school when they face adversity. It takes a great deal of determination to hang in there when things don't go according to plan.

In his "Last Lecture", the late Randy Pausch eloquently described life as "a series of brick walls" that are put in front of people to keep those who don't want success badly enough *out*. What are some of the "brickwalls" that you expect to encounter while getting your degree?

_____

_____

_____

Stamina

The third necessary element of effort is stamina. Stamina relates to how long a person can persevere under difficult or challenging circumstances. The classic examples of people who possess stamina are marathon runners. Marathon runners persevere through pain and exhaustion to finish long and grueling races. Similarly, graduating from college requires that students remain firm and continue moving forward when conditions become difficult.

Studying for difficult exams and writing term papers requires that students put in time during which they may feel bored, tired, confused, and frustrated. Students with stamina have the ability to work through these negative emotions over long stretches of time to reach their academic goals. Some courses may require much more stamina than others depending on how challenging students find the material. Students who have difficulty with quantitative subjects such as math, physics, or economics will need more stamina to do well in those courses. Likewise, students who have a lesser aptitude for courses involving large amounts of reading and writing will need more stamina to achieve good results in those subjects.

Think about it

In the end, you will have classes that test your energy, determination, and stamina. What courses do you feel will require more effort, and how will you prepare yourself emotionally to get through these classes to achieve the results you desire?

_____

_____

_____

_____

_____

_____

_____

_____

_____

Hard Work Personal Policy

Please take a few minutes to think about and write down your personal policy commitments regarding [1] time and deliberate practice, [2] delaying gratification, and [3] level of effort. Please write down your commitments in the spaces provided below. Try to be as specific as possible.

Hard Work Variable	*Commitment Statements*
[1] time and deliberate practice	[1] example: "I will commit to spending 2 hours from noon to 2:00pm everyday studying for Chemistry"
[2] delaying gratification	[2] example: "I commit myself to refrain from leisure activities until after my Chemistry homework and test reviews are finished.
[3] level of academic effort	[3] example: "I commit to completing all Chemistry assignments on time even when the work is confusing and difficult to comprehend.

Understanding Quality

"Every job is a self-portrait of the person who does it. Autograph your work with excellence."

~ Unknown

What is a student? Students can be defined as self-employed knowledge workers who acquire and use knowledge to complete academic work assigned by educators. Students acquire knowledge by committing themselves to long periods of time reading, studying, attending lectures, deliberately practicing, and researching. Their primary job duty is to acquire knowledge and complete all academic work [assignments and tests] and to do so in a way that satisfies educator requirements. Therefore, academic quality is a measure of how well students meet the requirements of the educators reviewing their work. Academic quality is, in large part, an outcome of student commitment.

Educators use a variety of tools to assess the quality of student work including tests, quizzes, research papers, group projects, oral presentations, etc. Grades are measures of academic performance, [residual evidence of the percentage of error-free academic work submitted by students]. For example, a 75 percent grade means that the work had an error rate of 25 percent. The error rate is the reciprocal of the grade. High grades mean low error rates, while low grades mean high error rates.

What would your opinion be of a new car that did not start 25 percent of the time, or a garbage man who hauled away only 75 percent of your trash, or a waiter who got 25 percent of your order wrong? Would a 25 percent error rate be acceptable to you? In academia, a 25 percent error rate is passing.

Grades are measures of academic quality. They are evidence of commitment— or your willingness to expend time and energy at the exclusion of other activities, to meet your obligations to professors. High grades reflect high levels of academic commitment, while low grades reflect low levels of commitment. Grades are measures of commitment.

Please write down your GPA commitment statement in the spaces provided below.

Quality Variable	*Commitment Statements*
[1] desired GPA goal at graduation	[1] example: I commit to achieving a 3.5 GPA upon graduation.

To Sum Up

Unit 3 focused on commitment, which can be classified as activity-based trust.

At the beginning of Unit 3 we defined what commitment is and demonstrated graphically in a Venn Diagram the overlapping relationship between the three commitment variables: dependability, hard work and quality.

The first commitment variable you learned about is dependability. We defined dependability and also introduced an equation that describes the three dependability variables: showing up on time, being prepared, and being ready to perform. We also reviewed the four other reasons that dependability is critically important: safety, success, cost, and teamwork. In addition, you were asked to take a dependability self-assessment and commit to some dependability goals.

The second commitment variable that was discussed is hard work. You were also introduced to an equation for hard work that has three components: time and deliberate practice, delay gratification, and effort. You also wrote down your commitments for how hard you would work.

The last variable you learned is quality. You learned that quality is an outcome of commitment.

Unit 4
Coping

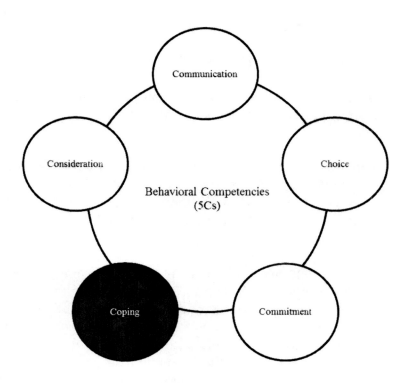

Understanding Coping

"Success is to be measured not so much by the position that one has reached in life as by the obstacles which he has overcome while trying to succeed."

~ Booker T. Washington

The choices we make during conditions of difficulty, pressure, or strain help shape the kind of people we become. Do we react before thinking? Do we let our emotions pull us in wrong directions? Do we become critical of and blame others when we are stressed? Difficult times test our ability to cope and help form our character. Helen Keller said, "Character cannot be developed in ease and quiet. Only through experiences of trial and suffering can the soul be strengthened, vision cleared, ambition inspired and success achieved." Difficult situations can create within us tension that makes demands on us physically, intellectually, and emotionally. The process of coping with such situations builds character.

With this as a backdrop, we can define coping as …

the ability to deal effectively with difficult or unpleasant situations.

Coping is problem solving during hard times. It is the ability to operate well in situations even when one is feeling frustrated, fearful, and stressed out. For that reason, coping is a situation-based trust trait.

Individuals who deal with difficult problems effectively can think clearly before they act or make decisions. They tend to be guided by their mind or intellect rather than their emotional reactions. To do otherwise, would be to put one's fate at the mercy of one's emotions. Things usually turn out much better when important decisions are not made on impulse, when one thinks before one acts.

Why is coping important? It's important because many of the problems we encounter in life will require that we work outside of our comfort zones. Physical, intellectual, and emotional growth happens most profoundly when we solve problems and cope successfully with situations outside of our comfort zones. When we cope effectively with situations that are new, unfamiliar, or unpleasant, we extend the reach and range of our understanding of the world in ways that more familiar and comfortable situations cannot. How can individuals grow if they only do that which they already know how to do? Coping involves operating in conditions that we may find painful and doing things that make us feel nervous or scared. These feelings are a natural part of coping. Any time you do something outside of your comfort zone, you too can expect to feel unsure of yourself. To develop more fully though, you need to push forward despite those feelings.

Successfully coping with difficult situations and problems is the foundation upon which true self-trust and self-esteem are built. True self-trust is grounded in one's ability to cope successfully with difficult problems. Students who can cope with the physical, intellectual, and emotional challenges they encounter in college develop true self-trust.

Finally, the more situations people can cope with, the more value they bring to society. People with college degrees who can solve difficult and complex problems are in high demand in today's world. Doctors, nurses, lawyers, engineers [civil, mechanical, electrical], computer scientists, senior executives, etc. are all well educated professionals that get paid well to solve specific types of problems. Remember, only about 30 percent of adults over the age of 25 years have a bachelor's degree or higher in the United States. The degree is evidence of, and a testament to, one's ability to cope.

In this unit, you will learn about coping by thinking in advance about change, adversity, and complexity.

Understanding Change

"He who rejects change is the architect of decay.
The only human institution which rejects progress is the cemetery."

~ Harold Wilson

According to the Law of Change[19], everything is continually in the process of becoming something else. Like death and taxes, change is impossible to avoid. Think about how the United States has changed over the last century. According to the U.S. Census Bureau, in 1910 the population of the United States was 92,407,000. Today, the population is 317,018,501 and growing. In 1910 only 13.5% of the population completed high school. Today, about 90% completes high school. In 1910, average life expectancy for men was about 48.4 years and women 51.8 years. Today, average life expectancy is about 75.6 years for men and 80.8 years for women. In 1910, Georgia, Missouri, Indiana, and Michigan had larger populations than California. Today, California's population is larger than all of those states combined. What will life be like in the year 2110?

It is hard to say for sure how the world will change, but we can say with certainty that it will change. If the world around us is changing, everyone should know how to cope with the problems and challenges associated with it.

Why can change be so difficult for people? Change is challenging because it forces people to cope with life outside of their comfort zones. To cope, one must be willing to accept or be patient with new and unfamiliar people, places, and activities. This push towards the unfamiliar can be hard for many people, and can make them feel uncomfortable, even scared. That's because often people are generally more comfortable and confident in their ability to succeed in familiar situations.

Think about it. When you operate within your comfort zone, and the people, places, and activities are familiar and predictable, it is usually much less stressful than when the people, places, and activities are unfamiliar or unpredictable. It takes courage to face the unknown. For some people, it may take a while before they can summon up enough courage to deal with their fears and embrace change. They may resist change if they sense that it will force them out of their comfort zones. In psychology, the term for this is *status quo bias*.[20]

To better understand what happens to new students psychologically and emotionally when they experience status quo bias, a colleague of mine asks new students a simple question. "What do you like better - variety or routine?" Many choose variety. Variety is fun and exciting. It is the

---

[19] Jack M. Balkin, "The Laws of Change - I Ching and the Philosophies of Life", Sybil Creek Press, 2009

[20] Kahneman, D.; Knetsch, J. L.; Thaler, R. H. (1991). "Anomalies: The Endowment Effect, Loss Aversion, and Status Quo Bias". Journal of Economic Perspectives 5 (1): 193–206.

"spice of life." Routines, on the other hand, can be dull and mundane. However, when asked to look around and notice where everybody is sitting week after week, they observe that everyone usually sits in the exact same seat. Some students even get upset when someone is sitting in *their* usual chair. People may seek variety for some things - food, music, restaurants - but people often cling tightly to their basic routines.

Routines are the familiar ways individuals perform their daily rituals and chores. They help us to process efficiently repetitive daily activities. Like cruise control, routines make life easier by taking the thinking out of doing the recurring things that we do. Individuals form routines over time, and like habits they can be very difficult to break. College will interrupt many of your routines and no matter how beneficial college may be for you, you should expect to feel uneasy because you will be giving up your old way of doing things … your old routines. Your feelings can run the gamut from being a little nervous and concerned, to full-blown anxiety. It's important to realize that these feelings are mostly normal, because you are giving up something that you value: the comfort and familiarity of your old routines.

To complicate matters further, you may not know anybody at college, which means that you won't know whom you can and cannot trust. Trust is built over time, so you should expect to feel mistrustful of the new people that you meet until you get to know them. When you combine feelings of uneasiness brought about by changes in routines, with the lack of trust, you may feel a bit overwhelmed, and may even say to yourself, "This isn't for me." Even the best students can expect to feel this at some point in college, and it may take a bit of time for those feelings to go away. These uncomfortable feelings may be a natural consequence of transitioning to college. Most students will be able to cope with these feelings as they make the transition to college, but some may not. They may not be emotionally or psychologically ready to make the transition to college.

Some students do not understand that many of their daily routines will need to change when they enter college. They bring their "high school mentality" into college and do the same things that they did in high school, because that's what they know. Please list below some of the ways college may change your routines.

_____

_____

_____

_____

_____

_____

Student Readiness for Change

As discussed earlier, entering college brings new students face to face with unfamiliar people and situations that they need to cope with. Some will embrace the change immediately and some will accept it over time, but others may never fully adjust.

The Department of Education estimates that 30 percent of college students leave school after the first year. Many of these students do not return because they were unable or unwilling to cope with change. Although increasing college costs, socio-economic inequalities, financial pressures, child care needs, and other factors can play a role, many students simply drop out because they do not cope well with the changes college requires. They may not even realize that when making the transition to college, it is normal to feel uncomfortable, confused, and at times, overwhelmed.

We can refer to the varying degrees of emotional and intellectual readiness that new students bring to college as "change readiness" or "transitional readiness." To help explain student readiness for college, let us look at an adapted version [Figure 4.1] of the Beckhard/Harris change model.[21] The model shows that the three variables on the left-hand side of the equation must outweigh the perceived cost of the change in order for the student to transition well into college. If the product is less than the perceived cost to the student, then a student may not be ready to change.

Student Readiness Change Model

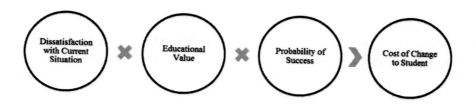

Figure 4.1

A student changes most readily when the product of the following situational elements are greater than the perceived cost of the change to the student:

1. his or her dissatisfaction level with current situation
2. how much the student values his or her education
3. the student's own perceived probability of success

---

[21] Richard Beckhard, Reuben T. Harris, "Organizational Transitions: Managing Complex Change", *Addison Wesley Publishing Company*, 1987

Student costs may include physical and emotional tolls, financial expenses, disruption of current lifestyles, and opportunity costs. If any of the model variables on the left side of the equation are low, the chance for a successful transition to college is lowered significantly. Similarly, if the costs to the student are too high, there is also less of a chance of a successful transition.

Think About It

Please answer the following questions. [Circle Yes or No]

1. Are you dissatisfied with your current situation outside of school?   Yes or No
   [e.g. financial, work, home, friends, car, etc.]

2. Do you see a direct benefit to you in getting a college education?   Yes or No
   [e.g. transfer or graduate schools, promotions, career, etc.]

3. Do you think that you can be successful at college?   Yes or No
   [e.g. intellectual difficulty, balancing work and home obligations, financial, time, behavioral, etc.]

According to the Beckhard/Harris Model, if you answered "No" to any of the above questions, you may need some time to make the transition to college. In the space provided below, please explain your "No" answers. What might you do to change these "No" answers into "Yes" answers?

_____

_____

_____

_____

_____

_____

_____

_____

_____

Phases of Change

In 1969, Elizabeth Kübler-Ross first introduced the world to what happens when people receive news that they are fatally ill.[22] As you can imagine, this type of catastrophic news profoundly effects people, and stirs up intense emotional reactions. What Kübler-Ross found was that the way that people react to this type of news is actually predictable. She said that people typically experience five emotional stages that are referred to as the "5 Stages of Grief": denial, anger, bargaining, depression, and acceptance.

Just try to image a doctor and a nurse coming into your examination room, they close the door behind them, and they say, "We are sorry, but you have inoperable pancreatic cancer and you only have 6 months to live". How would you react? What Kübler-Ross said was that you would react in very predictable ways. She discovered that you may first be in denial. You might say to yourself, "This isn't happening to me." After some time passed, you might then move out of the denial stage and into the anger or bargaining phases. In these phases, you might become very angry and lash out at the world, or become scared, and try to negotiate or bargain with your God for clemency. After more time passed, and neither anger nor prayer worked to slow the progression of your illness, you might move out of the anger and bargaining stages, and slip into the depression stage. Finally, towards the end, you might want to make peace with the world, so you might grow to accept your fate.

Kübler-Ross's insights can also help explain how people will react to other, less traumatic changes or transitions that people experience. As we discussed at the beginning of this section, when new students enter college many aspects of their lives change. Their routines usually change, and they may not know anybody. In addition, they may be struggling financially and may not be confident academically. Having to cope of with all of these changes, upheavals, and unknowns would make anyone feel anxious, confused, and even overwhelmed. It may be especially difficult for young people who are stepping out into the world by themselves for the first time.

We can use the Kübler-Ross model to help explain what happens to many students psychologically and emotionally when they enter college.[23] But instead of using the denial, anger, bargaining, depression and acceptance terminology used in the original model, we will simplify the model using only four terms to describe the typical ways that students react to college: *denial, destruction, discovery, and demonstration.* For our purpose, we can call this the "4 Stages of Student Grief" Model [see Figure 4.2].

---

[22] Elizabeth Kübler-Ross, "On Death and Dying," *Scribner*, 1969

[23] The Kübler-Ross model is widely used in business and change management and there are many variations and adaptations of the model that help predict and manage behavioral reactions to change.

4 Stages of Student Grief Model

Figure 4.2

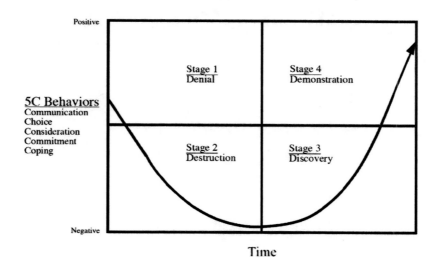

As Figure 4.2 shows, the 4 Stage Student Grief Model is a four-quadrant model that can serve as a conceptual framework for understanding what happens to many students when they enter college. Each quadrant represents a particular way students might react to college. When students come into college, they can react in one of three predictable ways. They can either:

1. Accept the change and immediately go to *Stage 4* and demonstrate that they understand what is required of them in college. They "walk the walk and talk the talk." They communicate appropriately, make good choices, commit to academic excellence, treat others with respect, and cope effectively with the rigors of college.

2. Accept change over time, which means they might initially behave in ways that are antithetical to their own academic interests. They might take some time to cycle through some or all four of the four stages. [denial, destruction, discovery, and demonstration]. For a period of time, they might make poor choices and communicate inappropriately, appear less committed than they should be, appear indifferent or even antagonistic, and appear to be unable to cope effectively with what is required of college students. However, after a while, the students who are willing to change will ultimately end up in Stage 4.

3. Reject college altogether and never adapt to the change.

Keep in mind that the stages can overlap, exist simultaneously, or be experienced out of order. With this model, we can actually predict how students will react to change, and see who is adjusting well and who is not. Let's take a look at each stage.

Stage 1 - Denial

Students in the *Denial* stage do not demonstrate much, if any, interest in learning. They typically act like none of the material being taught is important or applies to them. As they begin to realize that their old way of doing things doesn't work, they may begin to act in ways that are antithetical to the 5Cs. They might make poor choices about their levels of commitment and/or consideration, and may demonstrate signs that they aren't coping.

What types of behaviors would you see that would identify students who are in denial? What would you hear and/or see?

_____

_____

_____

_____

_____

Stage 2 - Destruction

Students in the *Destruction* phase actively resist the educational process. They behave in a way that communicates that they are not coping with what is required of a college student. They make poor choices and their levels of commitment and consideration fall dramatically. They behave in an antagonistic way and in doing so fail to accept or comply with accepted behavioral norms. They seem very unhappy.

What types of behaviors might you identify in students who are in the Destruction phase? What would you hear and/or see?

_____

_____

_____

_____

_____

Stage 3 – Discovery

In the *Discovery* phase, students begin to realize that they can handle the work. They might experience some success, which will give them feelings of hope, confidence, and courage. They begin to cope and start to take risks in class. It is as if a light bulb turns on and they begin to see what is in the darkness. They have a higher level of commitment, consideration, and energy in class. They start to smile.

What types of behaviors would you see that would identify students who are in the Discovery phase? What would you hear and/or see?

_____

_____

_____

_____

_____

Stage 4 - Demonstration

The final phase is *Demonstration*. In the demonstration phase, students know that they can cope with the rigors of college. They know what they need to do, and they demonstrate student success. They may start to help out their fellow students, and may already be thinking about next semester or life after college. They are purposeful, confident, committed, and considerate. What types of behaviors would you see that would identify students in the Demonstration phase? What would you hear and/or see?

_____

_____

_____

_____

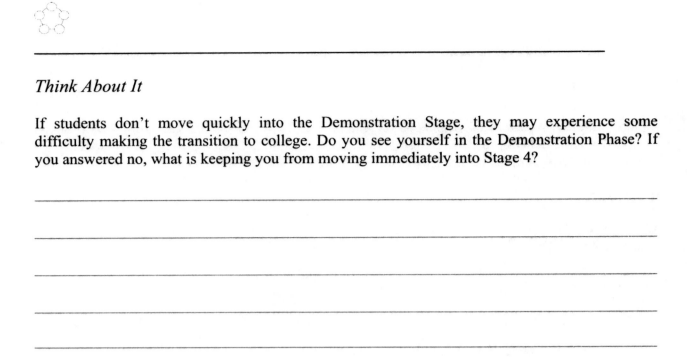

Think About It

If students don't move quickly into the Demonstration Stage, they may experience some difficulty making the transition to college. Do you see yourself in the Demonstration Phase? If you answered no, what is keeping you from moving immediately into Stage 4?

_____

_____

_____

_____

_____

Understanding Adversity

"The road to success runs uphill."

~ Willie Davis

The job of being an effective college student has always been difficult. There have always been demanding professors, overly competitive students, high tuition and book costs, complex subjects, unreasonable deadlines, too much material to memorize, lazy team members on group projects, illness, and so on. You may experience some of these problems yourself. In the event that you do, it is helpful to plan out *in advance* the behavioral strategies you will use to cope with the problems you experience. Many students get frustrated and react negatively when things do not go their way. They may drop out rather than cope with the problems they encounter. The fact that only about 30% of the adult population in the United States over the age of 25 has a bachelor's degree or higher, is evidence of the difficulty of the undertaking.[24]

Ultimately, coping with adversity requires an understanding of and belief in one's self. Every person will have problems that he or she alone must cope with. In general, students who are best able to handle adversity possess a set of behavioral qualities that enable them to overcome the problems they face. The qualities that help people understand and stabilize their behavior during difficult times are self-awareness, self-restraint, and self-improvement.

Self-Awareness

"That is the hardest thing of all. It is much harder to judge yourself than to judge others. If you succeed in judging yourself, it's because you're truly a wise man."

~ Antoine de Saint-Exupéry

None of us is as self-aware as we would like to be. We are all unique. Understanding our uniqueness, including our own behavior during difficult times, is an important part of developing a strategy for how to cope with problems you will face in the future. Are you usually good under pressure, or do you have a tendency to get angry, upset, or disengage in some way that may undermine your own effectiveness? Do you blame others when things go wrong? Do you take responsibility for your own actions? Without an accurate understanding of one's own predispositions (i.e., how we think and act during times of adversity), it is hard to cope with difficult situations effectively.

---

[24] United States Census Bureau, Educational Attainment in the United States: 2011 - Detailed Tables, http://www.census.gov/hhes/socdemo/education/data/cps/2011/tables.html

We can define self-awareness as ...

an accurate understanding of oneself, including one's own
values, traits, feelings, and behaviors during difficult situations.

How can you make good decisions about how to react to a situation, if you do not have a clear understanding the type of person that you want to be? How would you know how to judge the appropriateness of your behavior if you did not have any standards for your behavior? The ability to correctly prioritize important matters in front of unimportant matters during times of adversity requires self-awareness and behavioral understanding. It is at these times, at these decisive moments, when self-awareness and behavioral understanding are most important. Without this understanding, clarity of judgment is very difficult.

Describe a moment when your reactions helped you resolve a problematic situation. What did this teach you about yourself? What were the things you did well?

_____

_____

_____

_____

_____

Next, describe a moment when your reactions hurt your ability to resolve a problematic situation. How would you change the way you reacted to achieve a better result?

_____

_____

_____

_____

_____

Self-Restraint

"The beauty of the soul shines out when a man bears with composure one heavy mischance after another, not because he does not feel them, but because he is a man of high and heroic temper."

~ Aristotle

Coping effectively with difficult situations [i.e. solving problems without hurting oneself or others in the process] communicates a great deal about your ability to handle pressure. Self-restraint helps take the emotion out of solving difficult problems, which makes it easier to clarify the nature and meaning of situations, and thereby improve reasoning and judgment. People who cope well with adversity "maintain their cool," when the going gets tough. They do not "throw a fit" every time something goes wrong in their life, and are able to maintain a calm and steady control over their emotions.

Self-restraint can be defined as …

the ability to cope successfully with one's inner emotions, desires, and tendencies during stressful situations.

Self-restraint requires you to work consciously through anxious feelings without acting on impulse, or behaving in angry or unreasonable ways towards others. Self-restraint is particularly hard when you are emotionally close to a situation. According to Professor John Bunnell, "true self-restraint is *keeping one's cool* when one is immediately affected by a situation."[25] Human beings are not machines. Each of us has "lost our cool" at one time or another and acted in incorrect, unwise, or unfortunate ways that we may regret. That is part of being human. When losing control of one's emotions is a standard way of behaving, patterns emerge that communicate a lack of proper regard for the needs, wishes, and feelings of others.

Self-restraint is good personal policy in almost every circumstance. It allows clarity when we are coping with important issues and making crucial decisions. Exercising self-restraint demonstrates that we have guiding principles or personal policies that inform our own behavioral decision-making during difficult times. Examples of personal policies for self-restraint might include, "I will try not to take things personally"; or "I will always try to maintain my composure when facing adversity"; or "I will never punch another person with my fists or my words." There are many others. Without defined standards for self-restraint, any behavior may appear to be okay. Without predefined personal policies, human beings are capable of great harm.

Are you in control of your emotions or are your emotions in control of you? Please take a few minutes to think about and write down your own set of self-restraint personal policies, which will help guide your behavior during difficult times.

---

[25] John Bunnell, Professor, *SUNY Broome Community College*, Binghamton, New York, 2012

1. Establish a behavioral stretch goal for yourself in all matters. Stretch goals are long-term goals that you seek to attain. They can help clarify the rightness or wrongness of your thinking and behavior during times of adversity and serve as an example or rule to live by. They should be short and limited to one sentence [e.g., "I am committed to handling _all_ matters with grace or dignity."].

_____

_____

_____

2. Establish a "zero tolerance" personal policy for yourself regarding loss of self-restraint. Zero tolerance policies eliminate ambiguity that could cloud your judgment and decision-making during stressful times. For example, "It is _never_ okay to pull the car over and attack another person" is an example of a self-restraint policy that provides clarity for behavioral options in times of extreme stress while driving. Physical assault is not an option in any setting, except in the most extreme of unsafe circumstances. A less dramatic "zero tolerance" policy might be, "I will always maintain my cool and not damage others, even when I am under pressure and things do not go my way." These policies remove the behavioral guesswork when confronted with difficult emotional situations. What are the types of self-restraint personal policies one might adopt in an academic setting?

_____

_____

_____

3. Employ stress reduction techniques to gain control and reduce your tension during difficult times. Are there any techniques you use when you are about to lose your composure?

_____

_____

_____

Self-Improvement

> *"The farther a man knows himself to be free from perfection, the nearer he is to it."*
>
> ~ *Gerard Groote*

Nobody is perfect. Everyone has shortcomings that can be improved in some way. This is particularly true for coping. Coping with adversity is a difficult skill to master thing, especially when it immediately affects you.

For our purposes, we can think about self-improvement as …

> *a life-long process of bettering one's own nature, abilities, and character*
> *by one's own efforts during stressful situations.*

To improve coping skills, we must critically and honestly examine our own thoughts, emotions, behavior, and motivations *after* difficult events have passed. We need to continually evaluate our own behavioral performance against our personal policies and behavioral standards. Again, this presupposes that one has predefined standards against which to measure one's performance. Was my behavior in alignment with my predefined behavioral standards, or did I fall short in some way? Without an honest evaluation of our own behavior following difficult times, we might not know if our approach to coping was effective.

Improving your ability to cope can be difficult due to the painful emotions and feelings that accompany tough times. For that reason, you need to have the emotional and intellectual strength to endure hardship, accompanied by the desire to improve your own reactions to adversity. Without a willingness to cope with difficult emotions, improving ones ability to cope with adversity is almost impossible. Life continually tests our ability to cope. As my mother used to say, "You gotta wanna."[26]

Have you ever behaved in a way that you did not like? If so, what was the behavior, and did you commit to improving the behavior after you realized it was wrong? If not, why not?

_____

_____

_____

_____

---

[26] Kari Bonini-Roma, *Artist and Mother of four children*, 1937-1996

Understanding Complexity

One of the primary responsibilities of students is to demonstrate that they can handle the complexity of college. Can you handle the workload required for each course? Can you handle the combined workloads for all of your courses? Do you have complete understanding of the course material, or has the course complexity hampered your comprehension in some way? Can you balance all of the academic and nonacademic activities that you encounter in college?

Professors assess student academic work to determine whether or not their students understand and can cope with the level of academic complexity in their courses. Tests, quizzes, homework, oral and written reports, and class participation all measure the student's ability to cope with academic complexity. Most good professors will stretch their students to determine how much complexity they can handle before they fall behind. Specifically, most professors will stretch their students to find out their capability [what students know] and capacity [how much work students can handle] levels.[27]

Capability

Capability is an assessment of one's ability to comprehend the subject matter. Is the level of comprehension complete, or is it incomplete? Capability is not solely a function of one's intellectual smarts. It is more than that. Good grades and academic understanding rely heavily on one's behavioral choices. Student behaviors, i.e. studying, showing up for class, putting in time to do homework, and delaying gratification, all influence student performance. Students, who study and go to class, learn more and perform better than students who do not.[28]

Academic capability relies on behavioral performance, and grades represent student proficiency in both areas (academic and behavioral). As discussed earlier, grades are measures of academic excellence, residual evidence of the percentage of error-free academic work submitted. In essence, grades are a measure of academic capability. For example, a 75% grade means that the student capably handled 75% of the questions, with an error rate of 25%. High grades mean highly capable, while low grades translate to a lower level of capability within that subject area.

One of the best ways to cope with courses that are difficult conceptually is to put together a workable plan to manage this complexity. A plan might include answers to the following questions:

- Can I space difficult classes out over several semesters so that I am not taking too many difficult courses at the same time?

---

[27] adapted from Joseph Cadwell, Leadership Skills for Managers: American Management Association, 2004, p.71

[28] Gian Paolo Roma, Self-Management: Understanding Behavioral Competency, Friendsville Publishing Group, createspace.com, 2014, Appendix I, p.40

- Can I take the course in the summer?
- When I do not understand something, how will I get answers to my questions?
- Is the professor approachable if I have questions?
- Can I use the Learning Assistance Center or hire a tutor?

Capacity

Professors also assess student capacity. Capacity is a measure of the quantity of work a student can handle before knowledge acquisition begins to erode. Textbooks are thick for a reason. Many textbooks and courses contain content-rich vocabularies of technical terms. Every field of study from science, to accounting, to history, to nursing to philosophy has its own language. The languages may not be conceptually difficult to understand, but they may require learning many new terms.

Think of capacity this way: If you had to parachute into Russia, it would be a good idea to speak Russian. If you did not speak Russian, you would not be able to get around as well as if you spoke the language. When professors seem to be assigning too much work, they are trying to increase your capacity in their courses. Capacity, like capability, relies heavily of behavioral performance [i.e., putting in time and effort required to get through large quantities of subject matter].

Coping with the complexity [capability and capacity] of college requires behavioral competency. Can you handle the complexity of the course that you have taken? Have you been putting in the time and effort required to cope with the complexity of college? If not, why not?

_____

_____

_____

_____

_____

_____

_____

In the end, whether or not your professors are unreasonable, you will still need to get through their classes. Complaining about a professor is not coping. You need to proactively develop a plan that will help you manage the complexities you face in college.

Commit to These Quick Tips for Coping

- Get your ego out of your interactions with others
- Don't take things personally
- Memorize and practice your personal policies so that they become automatic
- Be considerate to others
- Be more patient
- Take emotions out of situations
- Get proper perspective on things
- Value others and try not to judge
- Accept responsibility for problems that you may have created
- Apologize when necessary to those that you have harmed
- Be honest with yourself about your own behavior
- Understand and accept that problems are part of life
- Don't blame others especially when you are the cause of a problem
- Forgive others for their mistakes
- Be considerate even when you don't want to be

Other Quick Tips

_____

_____

_____

_____

_____

_____

_____

To Sum Up

In Unit 4, you learned that coping communicates one's ability to deal with difficult situation, and for that reason, is characterized as the situation-based trust trait. We reviewed three situations that you should be able to recognize and cope with: change, adversity, and complexity.

In the change section, you learned how hard it is for people to change their routines. You learned that change forces people out of their comfort zones, which creates fear in people. You were introduced to the term status quo bias.

Second, you were introduced to two change models: the Student Readiness Change Model and: the 4 Stages of Student Grief Model. You were asked to think about where you see yourself relative to each model.

Third, you also learned important behavioral qualities that enable people to cope with adversity: self-awareness, self-restraint, and self-improvement. You were asked to think critically about how you handle adversity in your life, and to write down some stretch goals to help guide your decision-making during challenging times.

Fourth, we discussed strategies to help you manage complexity in your life. Specifically, you learned the difference between how capable you are and the amount of capacity you can handle. Lastly, you reviewed some "Quick Tips" for coping with change, adversity, and complexity.

Unit 5
Consideration

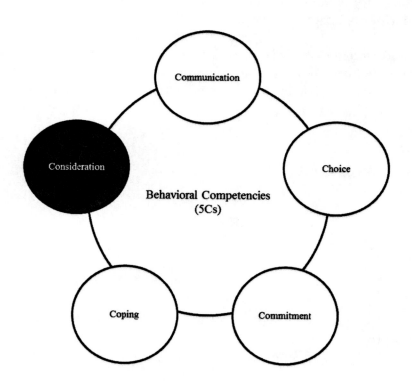

Understanding Consideration

"Intensely selfish people are always very decided as to what they wish.
They do not waste their energies in considering the good of others."

~ Ouida

When individuals interact with each other, they form connections. The connections can be strong or weak depending on the nature of the interactions. The context of the interactions affects the connections and defines the roles of the people involved and how they participate. Participation can range from warm, friendly, and sincere, to unfriendly, antagonistic, and disingenuous. This is true for interactions with family, friends and coworkers, as well as cashiers, customer service personnel, on-line help, police officers, professors, and anyone else. Regardless of the context in which individuals interact, conduct and attitudes that undermine another person's dignity, confidence, and self-worth will always weaken or possibly even sever the connections that bind people together. Interpersonal exchanges connect one person to another. Considerate exchanges strengthen connections, while inconsiderate exchanges weaken connections.

Good relations with others rely on an unspoken assumption that all parties are mutually interested in each other's well being. If an individual communicates [verbally or nonverbally] that he or she does not care about another's well-being, then the other party is not likely to care in return. Although not rocket science, many intelligent and well-educated people do not seem to grasp this basic concept. Theodore Roosevelt summed it up: "Nobody cares how much you know, until they know how much you care."

The main problem with inconsiderate behavior towards others is that it weakens or destroys the cooperative spirit and goodwill in people. Individuals that are treated poorly will show little, if any, willingness to assist or engage with inconsiderate people. Although hard work may put you in a position to be successful, it's thoughtful consideration towards others that will make them want to associate with and support you.

Consideration is most important in situations that depend on cooperation between people, because it makes cooperative relations between people possible. Alexander Graham Bell once said, "Great discoveries and improvements invariably involve the cooperation of many minds." Bell understood that one individual working alone could not invent the light bulb or construct a satellite, aircraft carrier, skyscraper, or highway. One individual cannot possess all of the knowledge, skills, and abilities, or master all of the complexities required to complete undertakings such as these. However, thousands of individuals working together cooperatively over time, have made possible the seemingly impossible.

If Bell's insight into the importance of cooperation is accurate, and inconsiderate behavior destroys people's willingness to cooperate, then it is vitally important for people to understand what considerate behavior is and is not.

Consideration can be defined as ...

a thoughtful concern for others that strengthens trust and cooperation between people.

We can try to understand considerate behavior by comparing the degree to which an individual shows concern for others versus concern for oneself [Figure 5.1].

Consideration Model

Figure 5.1

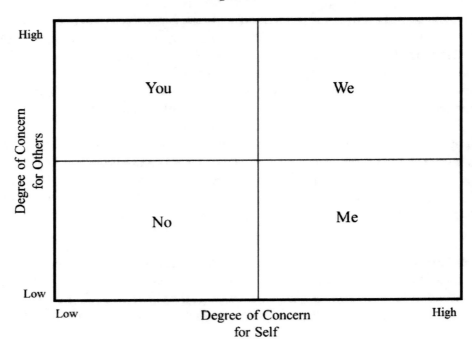

If people show a high degree of concern for others they are considerate. As the grid shows, individuals that demonstrate a high level of concern for others have either a *"you"* or a *"we"* orientation. The distinction between "you" and "we" depends on the degree of concern the person shows for oneself.

A person that demonstrates a high degree of concern for others and a high degree of concern for oneself would be we-oriented. A we-oriented behavioral approach tries to balance one's own wants, needs, and desires with that of other people they interact with. In general, we-oriented individuals work hard at relationships, and try to make sure that all parties [oneself and others] feel like they are treated fairly when interacting. By contrast, individuals with a "you" orientation would have high levels of concern for others, but low levels of concern for oneself. You-oriented individuals would subjugate their own needs to those of others.

Inconsiderate behavior, which is at the other end of the "Concern for Others" spectrum, shows a low degree of concern for others, and is labeled on the chart as having either a "no" or a "me" orientation. The distinction between a "no" and "me" orientation would again depend on the degree to which the behavior shows concern for oneself. We can describe a "no" orientation as being indifferent or unconcerned about the outcomes of people's behaviors on themselves or others. In general, no-oriented people would view the outcomes of their own behavior as being an unimportant consideration in their dealings with others. Me-oriented people, on the other hand, would demonstrate a low level of concern for others, but a very high level of concern for themselves in their dealings with others.

What do you think?

What types of behaviors would people exhibit in the different quadrants? What quadrants do your associates, friends, and relatives fit into? What quadrant do you fit into?

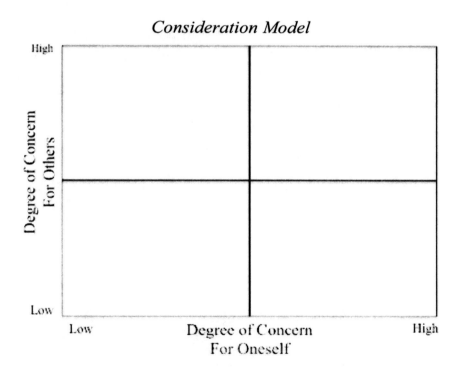

Consideration Model

As you can see, consideration is not a deep emotional understanding of another's feelings or problems. Rather, it is recognition that all people are worthy of respect, and that we should strive to treat each other in a dignified manner. Without consideration, *genuine* trusting relationships with others are not possible.

As said throughout this book, everything you say and do communicates facts and information that influence how others see you. What and how you communicate helps others determine your underlying nature, and whether they want to associate with you. Consideration makes trusting, healthy, long-term relations with others possible. Consideration is a behavioral minimum, and can be categorized as the relationship-based trust trait.

There are a variety of behaviors that create goodwill and encourage cooperation in people. To be viewed as a considerate person, you should willingly:

1) listen and try to understand what is being communicated
2) be courteous and polite
3) be kind and respectful to others
4) be helpful to people who need assistance
5) consider negotiating to settle disputes

Take a look at each of these behaviors in detail.

Listening

"Listen or thy tongue will keep you deaf."

~ Native American Proverb

Considerate people listen to and are interested in what others are communicating. Their focus is outward leaning. Making an effort to listen in an interested way is not a hovering attentiveness; it is a predisposition to appreciate authentically the opinions and ideas of others. Considerate people try to grasp the significance of alternate [or opposing] points of view, because they understand how much they themselves may not know. Considerate people understand that nobody has all of the answers, even if they are really smart, really articulate, and well-educated.

Inconsiderate people do not listen to, or make an effort to understand what other people are saying. Their lack of interest stifles goodwill and cooperation between people. They communicate that what others are saying is not worthy of their attention. Inconsiderate people close off the connections that binds people together, by disregarding as unimportant, irrelevant, or untrue the opinions and ideas of others.

Quick Tips For Becoming a Better Listener:

Be Attentive: Focus your mind, ears, and eyes on the people with whom you are interacting.

Don't Interrupt: Let people finish talking before you start talking.

Ask Questions: Ask questions to show interest, find out more, or if you do not understand what is being said [verbally and nonverbally].

Stay on Topic: Don't change the subject; it implies a lack of interest in what is being said.

Be Patient: Think long-term instead of short-term. Healthy, trusting relationships with others may take a while.

Reply Back: Provide verbal and nonverbal feedback to let the speaker know you understand and are interested in what is being said.

Courtesy

"Really big people are, above everything else, courteous, considerate and generous -- not just to some people in some circumstances -- but to everyone all the time."

~ Thomas J. Watson

You cannot be viewed as considerate if you are not courteous. Courteous people are well mannered and polite, and are aware of how their behavior affects others. They try to avoid harm in their interactions with others. Courteous people wait, hold the door for others, use turn signals when changing lanes, say "bless you" when someone sneezes, or "thank you" when a waitress brings their food. They take the time to acknowledge respectfully the presence of others. "Life be not so short but that there is always time for courtesy," Ralph Waldo Emerson reminds us.

Inconsiderate people, on the other hand, are rude and impolite. They ignore, snub, denigrate, humiliate, or embarrass other people. They are deliberately hurtful and insensitive to the feelings of others, and create situations where others feel upset, angry, or embarrassed. Discourteous people make others feel unworthy of their respect.

Think About It

What are three examples of impolite behavior that you notice in others?

1. _____

2. _____

3. _____

Kind

"Be kind; everyone you meet is fighting a hard battle"

~ Ian MacLaren

Kindness is the ability to behave in a friendly and good-natured way towards others. Kind people are friendly and nice. They are approachable and respectful to: family, friends, other students, teachers, co-workers, bosses, bus drivers, truck drivers, etc. Kind people do not require anything in return in order to be nice. Mark Twain put it best when he said, "Kindness is the language which the deaf can hear and the blind can see."

While considerate people are kind when they interact with others, inconsiderate people are insensitive, and may treat others harshly. They are mainly concerned with their own desires, interests, needs and wishes, and tend to ignore the feelings of others. People who are treated unkindly may experience feelings of inadequacy, anger, hostility, and resentment. What can be gained by creating these feelings in others?

A former colleague of mine, who was an operations director at a major telecommunications company in California, once told me a story that illustrates how inconsiderate behavior poisons relationships..

> Two of my employees where arguing about a new corporate human resources policy. Although both of the employees reported to me, they were not on the same level. One of the employees was my secretary, and the other was an operations manager. They both reported directly to me.
>
> I can't remember what exactly they were arguing about, but the exchange was very public and very heated. Before it got too ugly, the secretary stormed off to get the policy to figure out who was right and who was wrong. When she returned, she waved the policy and very publically scolded the manager in front of everyone in the office, "I just went to HR and they gave me the policy statement. It say exactly what I said. I'm right. "
>
> At that point, the manager said, "Okay, you're right" and went back to his office. After a few minutes, I called the secretary into my office and asked her what had happened, and she told me the details of the argument, and said that, "she was right." Then, I said, "You might have been right, but you're *dead* right. You're now dead to Frank. Was it worth it?" She didn't understand what I meant.
>
> I explained that Frank could be her next manager, or evaluate her performance, or be on a hiring committee for a job that she may be interested in, or on a promotion committee. I continued to explain that although she might never report directly to

Frank, that he had influence on her position and if he was asked about what it was like to work with her he might not give her a good recommendation. He might not say anything, he might just roll his eyes, but his point would be made. I explained that opportunities could be lost for her because of this event and she'd never know why.

How do you think Frank will react to you the next time you need to interact with him?

I hope being right was really worth it?

The moral of this story is that other people don't really care if *you* are right or wrong. They do care about how they are treated. If you are interested in establishing and maintaining healthy, trusting, long-term relations with others, you will be friendly and nice. Relationships are more important than being right. A "we" orientation is preferable to a "me" orientation. Wayne Dyer puts it this way, "in terms of improving relations with others, it's better to be nice than right."

The other important lesson in this story is to never publicly denigrate, or openly treat another person like they are unworthy of your respect. Although they may forgive you, they will never forget. The communication axiom to remember is, "praise in public, criticize in private."

Thank About It?

Think of a recent interaction, [whether or not you were involved] in which you observed unkind behavior. What did you think of the person exhibiting the behavior? What reactions did you observe from others?

_____

_____

_____

_____

Helpfulness

Considerate people are helpful to others. They provide useful assistance when others are in need. To be helpful one should willingly provide support to others in ways that are appropriate to each situation. Helpful people are aware of and sympathetic to the plight of those around them. This helps create order.

Inconsiderate people bring disorder and confusion to situations. They lack sensitivity to the feelings of people who need help, and are unconcerned about the plight of those around them. They communicate that their personal needs and wishes are of paramount importance.

Think About It?

Consider the following scenario. You are walking in New York City after a snowstorm when you see a man trying to dig his car out and he looks exhausted. You notice three men in their twenties just standing back and watching the man struggle and doing nothing.

Is this You, We, Me, or No oriented behavior? Explain?

_____

_____

_____

_____

_____

_____

_____

_____

_____

_____

_____

Negotiate

"Things which matter most must never be at the mercy of things which matter least."

~ Goethe

To the Greek dramatist Sophocles there was "no greater evil than men's failure to consult and to consider" each other. Human beings that negotiate in good faith with each other demonstrate that they care about each other. When people show that that they care, they will be more likely to cooperate or settle disputes. Ultimately, if done well, negotiating creates goodwill, which can help you get what you want.

My late father-in-law once gave me a great piece of advice during a negotiation. He said to me, "Just make sure that when you are finished with the negotiation, everyone is happy." I call this *Murray's Rule*. To follow Murray's Rule, both negotiating parties do whatever they can to make sure that the opposing party is treated fairly during the negotiation. It's logical. If you show me that you care about what's important to me, I'll be more likely to care about what's important to you. Murray's Rule is "we" rather than "me" focused and uses considerate behavior as a tool in negotiating. We-oriented negotiating is "win/win," while me-oriented negotiating is at best "win/lose," and at worst is "lose/lose." As John F. Kennedy said, "You cannot negotiate with people who say what's mine is mine, and what's yours is negotiable."

Quick Tips for Becoming a Better Negotiator:

- Keep in mind Murray's Rule.
- Know what is most important to you and try to figure out what is most important to the other party.
- Remain considerate to the other party by actively listening and being courteous, kind, and helpful.
- Use disagreements with others as opportunities to practice negotiating. Problems you face with others are actually opportunities to develop negotiating skills that you will use throughout your life.
- Make offer statements or suggestions such as "How about if we"…, or "What if we try" …. if you are at an impasse.

Quick Tips for Considerate Behavior

Commit to showing people that you care with these behaviors:
- Have an interested and helpful manner.
- Memorize and write down your personal policies regarding your relationships with others
- Practice patience and forgiveness even if you disagree with their points of view
- Try to see the good in everyone
- Treat people like they are worthy of respect
- Use polite phrases such as please, and thank you, or would you mind if we tried this …

Be considerate even to the inconsiderate by trying to …
- limit your contact, if possible, with inconsiderate people [We all come into contact with such people at work, school, and other situations, but you don't have to seek out these personality types.]
- be aware of your demeanor and tone
- avoid aggressive and dismissive behavior
- address people with a respectful tone even when you don't agree or are feeling upset
- be silent if you do not think you can say anything positive
- be constructive and non-confrontational
- not get personal
- not make generalizations or assumptions about a person's character

When you do not want to be considerate try to …
- make small goals for yourself. For example, if you get impatient and upset in traffic, make a goal for yourself to not express anger at any driver today. [How? Imagine that they cut you off in traffic because they're rushing to the bedside of a dying friend.]
- remember that arguing about religion and politics is similar to getting into an argument with a New York City cab driver … you probably won't win.
- walk away when you're feeling like you are going to say or do something inconsiderate to another person.

If you are stressed or angry, try the following breathing technique:

Step 1 Close your eyes

Step 2 Inhale as deeply as you can four times. [Breath in through your nose and out through your mouth, slowly]

Step 3 On the fourth breath, hold your breath for 5-10 seconds, and then slowly let your breath out.

Step 4 Sit still and then open your eyes after half a minute.

To Sum Up

In Unit 5 we defined consideration as having thoughtful concern for others that strengthens trust and cooperation between people. You learned the reason why consideration is characterized as the relationship-based trust trait and that good relations with others may not be possible without it. We also discussed why considerate behavior is particularly important for gaining cooperation from people.

You were also introduced to a new Consideration Model and asked to describe some of the behaviors that would characterize the different orientations (We, Me, You, No).

Lastly, you learned about the five behaviors that create goodwill and encourage cooperation in people: listening with understanding; being courteous and polite; being kind and treating others with respect; being helpful to people needing assistance; and negotiating when appropriate.

APPENDIX I

Effect of Educational Attainment on Career Earnings and Employment

People entering the workforce without academic or technical proficiency are finding it more difficult to achieve their goals in today's increasingly competitive world. Decades of research has shown that over the course of their careers, college graduates are advantaged in two very important ways over their non-college counterparts: [1] they have much higher rates of employment, and [2] they earn much more money.

Let's first take a look at the relationship between educational attainment and rates of employment.

Education and Employment Rate

Each quarter, the U.S. Bureau of Labor Statistics publishes unemployment rate reports by educational attainment. The most current unemployment reports can be found at http://www.bls.gov/news.release/empsit.t04.htm. What are the current national unemployment rates for the population 25 years and over by educational attainment? Please summarize your findings in the table below.

Educational Attainment	Unemployment Rate
Less than a high school diploma	
High school graduates, no college (1)	
Some college or associates degree	
Bachelor's degree and higher (2)	

(1) Includes persons with a high school diploma or equivalent.
(2) Includes persons with a bachelors, masters, professional, and doctoral degrees.

As you can see, the unemployment rate for well educated workers is much lower than for workers with less education. That's because educational attainment is one of the most important factors used in making decisions about employment-related matters such as staffing and employee retention. This is particularly true in tight labor markets when unemployment rates are higher for all workers. When larger pools of well educated workers are available to work, employers can be more selective in whom they hire and keep, which increases unemployment rates for less educated workers.

The relationship between educational attainment and employment can be found in a report published by the U.S. Census Bureau. The report describes how those with more education are more likely to work full-time, year-round than those with less education. To see for yourself, please go to http://www.census.gov/prod/2011pubs/acs-14.pdf and complete the following table.

Educational Attainment	Employment Rate Full-Time, Year-Round Workers
None–8th grade	
9th–12th grade	
High school degree	
Some college	
Associate's degree	
Bachelor's degree	
Master's degree	
Professional degree (eg. engineer, lawyer, accountant	
Doctorate degree	

Source: Education and Synthetic Work-life Earning Estimates Report: Table 1 (September 2011)

What do you think?

If you were the owner of company and you received 325 resumes for five job openings, how would you sort the resumes before you began reviewing them, and would you look at all 325 resumes?

_____

_____

_____

_____

_____

_____

Education and Earnings

Although many factors affect how much money a person can make, one thing is clear: over a lifetime those with more education tend to earn a lot more money than those with less education. Education influences earnings in two ways: [1] as we have seen, people with more education spend less of their work-life unemployed, and [2] people with more education are in occupations that earn more money. According to the U.S. Census bureau report, "Education and Synthetic Work-Life Earnings Estimates" (2011):

> "Higher levels of education allow people access to more specialized jobs that are often associated with high pay. Degrees in many occupations are treated as job training that may be required for a position or earn the employee more pay within that position."

To see this for yourself, please go to http://www.census.gov/prod/2011pubs/acs-14.pdf and complete the table below with your findings.

Educational Attainment	Annual Earnings Full-Time, Year-Round Workers
None–8th grade	
9th–12th grade	
High School degree	
Some college	
Associate's degree	
Bachelor's degree	
Master's degree	
Professional degree	
Doctorate degree	

Source: Education and Synthetic Work-life Earning Estimates Report: Table 1 (September 2011)

Higher levels of education are required for many professions. Some jobs, such as lawyer, accountant, engineer, doctor, professor, and architect are impossible to get without the necessary educational credentials. Although there are no guarantees, a quick analysis of the data shows that for every year you invest in your education, the average return on the investment over a 40-year working is significant. Compared to the volatility of the stock and real estate markets, investing in your own education looks like a great bet.

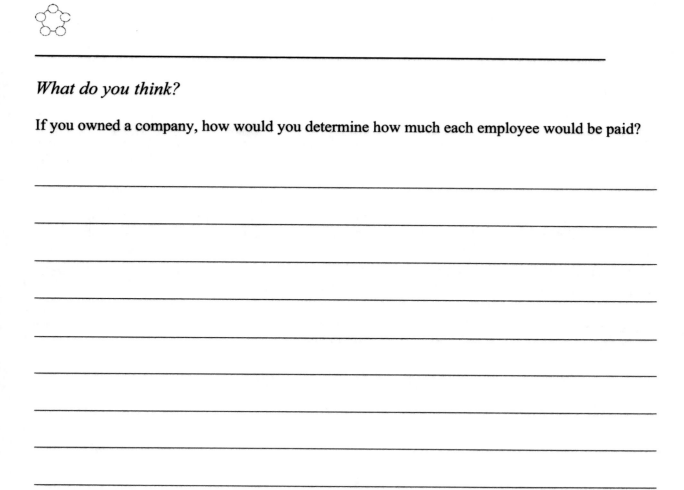

What do you think?

If you owned a company, how would you determine how much each employee would be paid?

_____

_____

_____

_____

_____

_____

_____

_____

To sum up

The consequences of not attending or completing college can be harsh. Employers are increasingly looking for employees who can contribute in a meaningful way to their organizations. They are searching for people with knowledge, skills, and abilities that can add value to their "bottom-lines."

Although there are alternatives to college for acquiring knowledge and developing skills, such as in technical and trade schools, a college degree remains a noteworthy achievement that society uses to make decisions about people. Many career opportunities are simply unavailable to those without a college degree. The degree is conclusive evidence that you have earned the opportunity to "dine at their table." What you do with that opportunity will be up to you.

The next variable in making good choices is accurately assessing your own situation. [See Appendix II - "Reality Assessment" – on the next page.]

APPENDIX II

REALITY
ASSESSMENT

External Reality
Worksheet

Instructions:

In a group, brainstorm and write down some of the general trends [opportunities and threats] in the following External Reality Worksheet. External realities are opportunities and threats that exist outside of each person.

- Opportunities and threats are mostly beyond an individual's control and generally difficult to change. Although an individual cannot do much to change external reality, he or she can proactively figure out ways to deal with such conditions.

- Opportunities are favorable conditions that exist for pursuing educational or employment opportunities.

- Threats are unfavorable conditions that could cause an individual trouble in college or career if not taken into account. How will the external reality affect your situation over the next few years?

- Write down your collective responses in the worksheet on the next page.

External Reality
Worksheet

Opportunities [Favorable circumstances that are advantageous to you]	Threats [Unfavorable circumstances that could be harmful if you fail to consider]

External Reality
Action Plan

Do any opportunities particularly appeal to you? What are the threats that most concern you? Please list the top opportunities, and the top threats that you believe will influence your own situation the most in the coming years. Then think about and write down what you need to do to take advantage of the opportunities, and minimize the threats that you identify.

_____

_____

_____

_____

_____

_____

_____

_____

_____

_____

_____

_____

_____

_____

_____

_____

Self-Management - Understanding Behavioral Competency
Friendsville Publishing Group
Gian Paolo Roma - © 2014 - All Rights Reserved

Internal Reality
Worksheet

Instructions:

Working alone, write down as many things that you can think of that are distinctive about you on the *Internal Reality Worksheet* on the next page. Internal realities are your unique set of strengths and weaknesses that exist within you.

- Strengths are things we do well or that work in our favor, such as strong computer, financial, foreign languages, work ethic, violin, sports, math skills, etc.

- Weaknesses, on the other hand, are the things that may inhibit our ability to achieve our goals, such as lack of dependability, no marketable skills, lack of financial resources, etc.

- To understand the role that your internal reality plays in your life, take a few minutes to jot down all the things you do well and things you may wish to improve.

Internal Reality
Worksheet

Strengths [Things you do well or that work in your favor]	Weaknesses [Things you don't do well or that inhibit your ability to do well]

What are your findings? What do you do well and where do you think that you need to improve? Are there ways that you can align your strengths with the opportunities that your group identified in the external reality worksheet? What are some strategies that you can employ to improve the areas of weaknesses that you identified?

_____

_____

_____

_____

_____

_____

_____

_____

_____

_____

_____

_____

_____

_____

About the Author

Gian Paolo Roma is an associate professor of Business Administration at SUNY Broome Community College. He teaches management, accounting, and student success courses.

Prior to teaching, Professor Roma was a member of the start-up team that launched Omnipoint Communications, the first GSM wireless carrier in Northeastern United States [now part of T-Mobile]. He led strategic planning, quality assurance, budgeting, workforce management, training, and project management for the customer service division. Prior to customer service, he managed regional and corporate marketing operations. Before the company launched, he established the company's handset and equipment warehousing and distribution operation, and designed the business requirements and managed the integration between the billing, point of sale/inventory, and warehousing and distribution systems. Before being acquired, Omnipoint grew to over two thousand employees and one million customers in only 3.5 years.

Professor Roma started his career at UNISYS and Singer-Link in Quality Assurance Engineering, before working for Texaco [now part of Chevron] and NYNEX Mobile Communications [now part of Verizon Wireless] in Corporate Communications.

He has a BS in Industrial Technology from the Watson School of Binghamton University, and an MBA from the Martino Graduate School of Business of Fordham University.

Publications:
Robert F. Hurley, Melissa Thau Gropper, Gianpaolo Roma, "The Role of TQM in Advertising: a conceptualization and Framework for Application", *Journal of Marketing – Theory and Practice,* Summer 1996, Vol. 4 No. 3

CPSIA information can be obtained
at www.ICGtesting.com
Printed in the USA
LVOW09s0027040117
519661LV00010B/106/P